Tamryn Kirby has been  expert' and was the founde
twice the winner of the title 'be
prestigious Wedding Awards and was responsible for over
250 weddings. Tamryn was the Style Editor for *Beautiful
Weddings*, a columnist for *Wedding Ideas* and diarist for
Wedding Professional, and has appeared regularly on TV
and on the radio, providing insight and expert commentary
on all wedding-related stories. Tamryn lives in Berkshire
with her son.

Confessions of a Wedding Planner

TAMRYN KIRBY

with Charlotte Ward

headline

First published in 2010
by HEADLINE PUBLISHING GROUP

1

Cataloguing in Publication Data is available from the British Library

ISBN 978 0 7553 6074 1

Typeset in Sabon by Avon DataSet Ltd,
Bidford-on-Avon, Warwickshire

Printed and bound in Great Britain by
Clays Ltd, St Ives plc

Headline's policy is to use papers that are natural, renewable and
recyclable products and made from wood grown in sustainable forests. The
logging and manufacturing processes are expected to conform to the
environmental regulations of the country of origin.

HEADLINE PUBLISHING GROUP
An Hachette UK Company
338 Euston Road
London NW1 3BH

www.headline.co.uk
www.hachette.co.uk

For my adored grandad,
Lawrence Douglas Eastment AFC

Contents

Acknowledgements

Huge thanks and beautiful (non-bridal!) bouquets to Carly Cook, my wonderful editor at Headline, and to Jane Turnbull, my fabulous agent.

Gigantic thanks and much love to the totally wonderful Charlotte Ward, without whom this book would not have happened, and it certainly wouldn't have been as much fun to put together.

Thanks to my amazing brides, especially those gorgeous and gracious women who made my job a joy.

To my favourite wedding planner, friend and top chef's missus, Julie Tooby. Here's to more greatness, more gossip and more evenings when the men are in the kitchen!

Thanks and love to my fab, caring and funny best friends – Debs and Julie, the best old biddies in the world. I hope we're still laughing loudly and leaving inappropriate things under tables for many years to come.

Mr K, regardless of what's passed, you are a truly wonderful father, a good friend, and I'll always be more proud of your achievements than of mine.

To my auntie – who would have thought that the blue bridesmaid's dress would start me off on this journey? Thank you for all the little doses of Cornish and French escapism that have kept me going over the past few years.

Darling Muv, there is nothing I don't have to say thank you for. You've taught me love, compassion and the benefits of doing your Christmas shopping in October. You are the most perfect mother anyone could wish for.

And lastly, to my Pippin with all my love. You are the most gorgeous boy inside and out. 'Mummy, when I grow up, I want to marry someone just like you. Only younger.' What more could I ever ask for?!

Prologue

We'd just finished the main course when the flamenco dancer arrived, in a flash of angry red lace. A Spanish guitar tune blasted out of an iPod as she pouted, stamped her feet and clicked her fingers, dramatically, if a little out of time.

As she strutted back and forth in front of the top table, the newlyweds smiled appreciatively, and the bride's mother clapped enthusiastically, bouncing in her chair.

The beat of the music grew faster and louder. All eyes were on the scarlet-clad dancer as she held her head up, brow furrowed with concentration, arms cutting precisely through the air, her heels pounding the floor.

All eyes except mine.

I was frozen to the spot, my steely gaze fixed on the wedding cake, on a stand just to the right of the top table. The mantra 'Please no, please no. Stop stamping!' rolled over and over in my head with each click of those castanets.

The cake was a glorious feast of towering glory, covered in creamy icing and topped with two dainty figurines of the bride and groom. A beautiful monument to wedded bliss, which was now swaying precariously as the dancer sent shuddering vibrations through the floor.

'That cake is going to go,' I whispered to myself, inwardly calculating how quickly I could navigate around at least a dozen tables to save it without taking out several guests in the process. From my position across the room, not quickly enough was the honest answer.

As I battled with this dilemma, thankfully the dancer came to a stop. With a final flourish of her fingers and a flick of her fringe, she bowed triumphantly and the room rippled with applause. The cake, I was relieved to see, was still intact.

'Thank God for that!' I exhaled, turning to my new (post-divorce) boyfriend, Matt, who seemed completely oblivious to what I'd been going through. I took a sip from my glass of champagne – and there was an almighty crash, causing everyone to jump in shock.

There on the floor was a mess of mashed sponge and icing, hardly recognizable as the gorgeous masterpiece that had been on the table just seconds earlier.

A ripple of gasps went around the room, and (inappropriately) some stifled laughter. Everyone was looking at the bride, whose serene glow had now been replaced with a look of thunder. If looks could kill, the flamenco dancer would have been a goner.

But there was just one emotion searing through me: immense relief that it was someone else's problem to sort out.

Twelve months earlier, it would have been me crawling around on the floor with a plate, napkins and a spoon, trying frantically to resurrect the sorry remains of a demolished cake, or standing in the loos handing the hysterical bride tissues.

During my five-year career as a wedding planner, I'd dealt with pretty much every scenario you could think of – among them, flashing brides, vomiting grooms and groping uncles. I've seen top tables set on fire, spied guests fainting, fighting and thieving, and witnessed mothers on the fast track to being disowned as they single-mindedly tried to sabotage their own child's wedding.

Of course, I've also attended many wonderful weddings where, like the guests, I've been swept up in the infectious atmosphere of love, goodwill and celebration. There's nothing quite like seeing a couple going gooey-eyed and holding hands as they both say 'I do'. Or seeing a couple who have been married themselves for fifty years sweetly waltzing on the dancefloor.

Then there are the moving scenes that unfold before your eyes, like the wedding where the gallant soldier rushed back from Iraq to be with his best friend on his big day. Or the determined and brave bride who, though terminally ill, summoned all her strength to walk down the aisle, her smile never faltering for a minute.

I've found myself struggling not to cry at tear-jerking speeches that couldn't fail to touch the heart of the most cynical guest. And I could never grow tired of the moving moment when a proud groom first sets eyes on his glowing bride.

I've come away with new friends and adorable god-children – an added bonus of planning weddings for radiant and lovely brides who I refused to lose touch with, and brides who are grateful for the trouble I've taken and understand the amount of skill and time involved in planning a wedding. It really is an art. I took pride in building up a successful business, which relied on word-of-mouth recommendations, won me great acclaim and several industry awards as well.

But I soon discovered that my job was far from the glamorous profession portrayed in films like *The Wedding Planner*.

Instead, I experienced first-hand the lunacy of utterly self-obsessed brides: the demanding divas quite fittingly labelled Bridezillas; the borderline anorexics who live on olives and carrot sticks, snapping or fainting at regular intervals; and the highly strung princesses who literally decide to cut friends from their lives because they fail to attend the hen weekend.

It may sound extreme, but you'd be amazed what wedding fever can do. While every bride wants her best pals to be there every step of the way, you have to pity the poor friend who is unable to afford time off work or the hundreds of pounds for a 48-hour jaunt to Ibiza.

Yet these days there is so much pressure heaped on brides it's easy to see why so many seemingly lovely ladies cross over to the dark side, becoming completely deranged in the run-up to their big day.

Competitive Wedding Syndrome can be nasty, as friends try their hardest to outshine their previously wedded girl pals with perfect venues, amazing entertainment and celebrity-style glitz and glamour. And when I started to pick up famous clients determined to have their wedding grace the cover of a weekly magazine, the competition was magnified tenfold.

The days of getting married in a small, humble ceremony, followed by a knees-up in the local church hall, are long gone. Now brides want it all – no matter what the cost.

The figures speak for themselves: the UK wedding industry is worth more than a staggering £4 billion every year, and the average wedding budget is over £20,000. A bride can easily spend 250 hours planning her big day, and the 'It's your day, have it your way' culture means that weddings are now expected to be more impressive, more original and more perfect than ever.

Stress levels rocket, relationships fall apart and some couples end up ignoring each other and barely communicating, or only through their wedding planner. It's far from ideal to see previously smitten lovebirds reaching their wedding day so uptight and unhappy that they have to be reminded to smile for the photographs.

Brides ban children from weddings in case they dare to make a noise during the vows, guests are told what colours to wear, and detailed information sheets are sent out with plans so regimented it would make an army general proud. It's an explosive combination, and when everything blows up, it's the wedding planner who will be standing right there in the fall-out zone.

Mercifully, it is also the wedding planner who can ease the burden and hold it all together, helping couples to have the wedding of their dreams, to enjoy the build-up almost as much as the big day, without any need for anxiety or a single cross word. The 'perfect' wedding does exist, and the good news is that anyone can achieve it and it has nothing to do with your budget.

But it's also time to put the myth of the 'wedding planner' to rest.

People believe our kind waft dreamily from cake-tasting to dress-fitting via an appointment at Tiffany's: this could hardly be further from the truth. The crashing reality of organizing other people's weddings is that you juggle an insane workload, at the cost of a complete lack of a private life. Even on snatched hours off, you are inundated with calls from demanding or hysterically emotional brides, interfering mothers and stressed grooms, never mind the last-minute hiccups, the ridiculous requests and the drunken relatives on the big day itself.

Part counsellor, part confidante, part conjurer and definitely a hundred per cent dogsbody, the wedding planner inhabits a strange world where big budgets and even bigger egos spiral out of control.

You might think it's a dream job but, ironically, the more successful I became, the more unhappy I was.

Towards the end of my career as a wedding planner, paranoia and depression crept in. I felt exhausted all the time and became addicted to surfing wedding forums in case I was being badmouthed by petty brides sniping over some tiny detail and determined to take their revenge in the most public way.

Behind closed doors, my own marriage was falling apart, and as I smiled and cooed over brides-to-be, my mind was filled with worries and woes.

So, in 2008, I got divorced and left my career behind. Then I started to pick up the pieces.

Looking back at my former career, I can now see things in a more positive light. I still love and respect the institution of marriage and everything it stands for. I have a little hope inside me that I might marry again one day, and I still get a real thrill from attending a lovely wedding and sharing that collective feeling of joy and excitement with the bride and groom. To see a couple happy, cherishing every minute of their big day with their family and friends – well, there's nothing like it.

The truth is, any bride can have the best day of her life, but it actually has little to do with the amount of cash you spend or whether everything goes off with military precision.

There's a lot that's lovely, and there can be a lot that's loathsome about weddings. I can tell you tales to make you laugh and cry, to inspire or horrify you.

We all have an inner Bridezilla waiting to bare her teeth, but it really doesn't have to be that way. If you're panicking about your own wedding, it's time to take a breather. Over the years, I have learned the secrets of the industry: I have more tips, tricks and problem-solving tactics than you could shake a bouquet at. And whether you're happily married, about to be or were once wed, I promise you there's plenty here to help you with your big day – and even if you're determined that you'll never marry, I'll certainly entertain you.

1.

An Early Obsession

The fairy tale carriage pulled up and, slowly, a beautiful bride stepped out in a puffball of ivory silk taffeta. She looked every bit a princess from a storybook, with her tiny bodice, hourglass waist and billowing skirt; the train seemed to go on for miles and miles.

Her face was covered by a veil, secured with a magnificent tiara, but as she glided down the aisle on her proud father's arm I could just about make out a coy smile. Shrieking with excitement, I jumped off the sofa and hurtled across the room to the telly, putting my nose as close to the screen as was possible without going cross-eyed.

I watched gleefully as Lady Diana Spencer took her place next to Prince Charles.

'You'd think they could have ironed her dress!' Mum commented from behind me.

The year was 1981, and I was just five years old.

For a little tomboy, I was surprisingly wedding-obsessed. Day to day, I could be found dashing about in jeans and T-shirts, climbing trees and racing on my bike. With my super-short hair and scabby knees, I was an unlikely princess-bride-to-be, but it was the whole spectacle of the royal wedding that drew me in. To a small girl, everything sounded so magical.

There was talk of Di's 'antique lace floor-length veil', the 'hand-appliquéd jewels' on her gown and her 'cascading lily bouquet'. Best of all, she was marrying *a prince*! It all seemed so out of the ordinary and impressive, yet now I knew that if a young nursery-school teacher could become a princess, then so could I! It was like being part of a wonderful story, the kind of thing my mum would read to me when she tucked me into bed every night. But this was real; we were all part of it. Fairy tales *did* come true – and who could possibly resist that?

I loved seeing everyone dressed up in gorgeous outfits, so soon I was collecting all the books, magazines and official memorabilia I could lay my hands on. Among my treasures were little Ladybird books on the royal weddings of Charles and Diana, and later of Andrew and Sarah Ferguson. While I enjoyed these books, I wasn't so keen on the historical wedding books that Mum also tried to tempt me with. These contained paintings and only the odd photo, and even in those everyone had stiff faces and didn't look very happy or very much in love! For me, it was the happiness and romance that Charles and Di, and Andrew and Fergie radiated that was the draw.

I have memories of even using my birthday money to buy wedding magazines. These always featured a beautiful model on the front cover wearing an equally beautiful dress.

'Planning your wedding already, are you, darling?' the

lady in my local newsagent's would chortle as I placed the stack of glossies on the counter.

I'm sure she thought I was bonkers, but it never fazed me. Instead, I'd dash home and pester Mum for some scissors and glue. Then I'd carefully cut out the pictures that I liked and paste them in my beloved wedding scrapbook.

I'd spend my time devouring the magazines, painstakingly redrawing the dresses, with huge skirts and lots of strapless bodices. Almost before I knew it, I was dressing up in Mum's gloriously seventies cream strappy heels and tottering around the garden with net curtain attached to my head, clutching a bouquet of garden flowers. And to my utter delight, I got to be a bridesmaid twice before the age of seven.

The first time was at the wedding of my Aunt Lorraine. My bridesmaid's dress was made from blue flowery fabric with a high collar and long sleeves, and I wasn't allowed to put it on until the very last minute, in case I got it dirty, which, given my track record, was a distinct possibility. Then, because I didn't have much hair, I was made to wear a skullcap, also covered in flowers.

During the service, an older bridesmaid (dressed in a distinctly less flowery dress than mine and also looking better without the skullcap) clutched my hand tightly and dragged me down the aisle. I thought my aunt looked like a princess, and seeing all my family dressed up was fabulous. I was also impressed that I was given a three-course meal and was then allowed to dance with the grown-ups.

Of course, years later, when I looked back at the photos, it transpired that my drab outfit and floral skullcap were every bit as hideous as you'd imagine – but they weren't nearly as bad as what my aunt was wearing. She'd walked down the aisle with a tight perm and white wooden wedge heels. In the grand scheme of things, I think I got off lightly.

My next bridesmaid moment, at the wedding of a second cousin, was very nearly stolen from me, because, selfishly, I'd broken my arm before the service. (Serves me right for wrestling the boys in the playground, though, doesn't it?)

Rather cruelly, there was much discussion about whether I was up to the job with my arm in plaster. Although I was told the adults were 'thinking about me', this was probably my first exposure to a slight Bridezilla moment: it was more about how a plaster cast would look in the photos. But with my cast removed in the nick of time, I was finally allowed my big moment. This time my dress was a tad nicer – a white and purple flowery number with a white lace underskirt and a purple velvet waistband and bow.

I can still remember the feeling of pride as I sashayed down the aisle behind the bride.

Over the years, my wedding fever never faltered.

I heard the wedding commentators panning Sarah Ferguson's cream A-line dress on the telly, and I also had opinions of my own. The huge bow wasn't something I'd have, but I loved the little bees which had been sewn into the train along with her initials. Her sparkly tiara was also divine. What I loved the most, though, was how Andrew and Fergie spent their entire wedding laughing and smiling.

The wedding even inspired me to write into *Jim'll Fix It* to ask if I could be picked up from school in one of the royal carriages. Unsurprisingly, I didn't hear a thing.

But the best was yet to come . . .

A TV wedding was about to capture the hearts of small girls, teenagers and grown adults everywhere. Scott was marrying Charlene on *Neighbours*! And it was the most romantic thing I'd *ever seen*.

The year was 1988 and, that day, it was all the girls in my year, and indeed the entire school, could talk about. Charlene was so pretty – even with that awful perm. Scott was so hunky – even with that disgusting mullet. Surely this was what dreams were made of?

As soon as the bell rang, I legged it home from school and positioned myself right in front of the TV. With my head tilted to one side and no doubt a gooey expression on my face, I marvelled at how Charlene, a bit of a tomboy like me, could look so pretty in her dress. And as 'Suddenly' by Angry Anderson blared out from the screen, I declared it to be the most romantic tune *ever*.

It was definitely the romance that enthralled me.

Being twelve and so approaching adolescence, I was completely caught up in the feeling that someone could love you so much they would ask you to marry them. Even now, I am still a complete romantic and a total sucker for a 'happy ever after'.

I'll always have hope that, despite everything, love will triumph, and that if someone loves you enough, you can do anything.

I'd love to say that after school and university I immediately fulfilled my heart's desire to be involved in weddings in some way, but in reality it didn't happen until I was twenty-seven. Before then, I tried a variety of occupations and spent some years in events management. So how did I become an organizer, fixer and miracle-worker for other people's nuptials?

Well, it was actually my own big day that first enticed me into the glitzy, romantic world of wedding planning.

My courtship with my husband-to-be, Michael, was hardly conventional.

I first met him on an internet dating site in April 2001, and by June I was pregnant with our son, Jake. Oops.

What can I say? We hit it off.

On our first date, Michael and I just talked and talked and discovered we had stacks in common. We just clicked and started seeing each other regularly.

In truth, I'd never expected to get pregnant. In my teens I'd been very ill with ME and ovarian cysts, and I'd been warned that the chances of my having a baby were slim. My illness had come like a blast from nowhere. I was fourteen, and ridiculously hyperactive. I loved sport and dashed around everywhere, yet suddenly I was too weak to even walk down the stairs. I had to give up netball, which I played for the county, as well as Air Cadets and all the outdoor pursuits I loved.

Over the next two years, the virus lingered on and then, on top of it all, just after I joined the sixth form, I was struck down with crippling pains in my abdomen. The pain was like nothing I'd ever experienced. It turned out I had cysts on my ovaries which had burst, and I was warned by my doctor that it would be difficult for me to become pregnant.

Yet a few years later, at the age of twenty-four, there I was, most definitely capable of having kids and most definitely pregnant by a man I'd known all of two months!

I'd always been completely regular, so the minute my period was late, I just knew. The facts spoke for themselves, and I was completely bloody terrified.

'What the hell am I going to do?' I groaned. 'I'm going to be a mother. Am I even maternal? What on earth will Michael say?'

That night I invited him round to the two-bedroom house I owned near Basingstoke. Thinking he might need the fresh air once I told him, I guided him into the garden.

'Um,' I started, biting my lip, 'I think I might be pregnant.'

I watched Michael swallowing hard, and he quickly plonked himself down into a garden chair.

'I don't know for definite yet,' I continued to gabble. 'I haven't done a test, but my period is late . . .'

By now Michael's face was as white as a sheet. I wondered if perhaps I should have stolen his car keys in a pre-emptive strike. But Michael, to his credit, didn't run, or demand to know why I wasn't on the Pill, or accuse me of entrapment. Instead, he held my hand, and attempted a weak smile. 'It'll be OK,' he told me calmly. 'But we should do a test as soon as possible to find out for sure.'

Then he stayed the night, hugging me tightly as I lay in bed wondering how on earth I'd cope with being a mother. I don't think either of us got much sleep, but it was such a relief to know that Michael was definitely on my side.

The next day I left for my job as a sales and marketing co-ordinator for a firm supplying company cars. I'd planned to do the test that night, and spent the morning staring into the screen at my spreadsheets and humming along to the radio, trying desperately to think about anything but the predicament I was in.

But by 12.30 I could stand the churning in my tummy no longer and rushed to the chemist's to pick up a test. Then I drove home and ran into the house and straight into the bathroom. My hands shaking, I quickly peed on the little white stick and awaited my fate. If it was positive, the little line in the middle would turn blue. I closed my eyes and tried to count to two minutes.

But I just couldn't wait. So I opened my eyes. It had already turned blue. I was most definitely pregnant.

Feeling slightly faint, I went back to work, and sat in a daze all afternoon. Michael came round that evening and got all the confirmation he needed as soon as he caught sight of the look on my face. His expression pretty much matched mine. We both looked like we'd been run over.

But once the initial shock had worn off, Michael was really calm and brilliant.

'It'll be fine,' he told me, a smile quickly expanding

across his face. 'We'll be happy. We'll get a place together!'

His enthusiasm was so infectious that soon I began to feel happy too. So what if it wasn't planned? I liked Michael, loved him even, and he could clearly see a future for us.

At no point did we discuss any alternative. I don't think getting rid of the baby was ever an option for either of us. Fate had decided we were going to be parents, and that was that. The following night, Michael came round with a baby book. We just got on with it.

The next hurdle, of course, was telling our parents.

I'd assumed my mum would be wonderful and my dad would need persuading, but it was completely the other way round. Mum was shocked and quite frosty at first, while Dad was brilliant. 'It's wonderful news,' he told me.

Mum came round in the end, though, even going out and buying all the baby books she used to read to me.

When the scans started, the reality hit. I was actually going to be a mum! And I soon realized I'd need all the help I could get.

There are so many girls on my mother's side of the family that I was utterly convinced I was going to have a little girl, but my twenty-week scan begged to differ. As I lay on the examination bed, my tummy covered in that awful sticky jelly, the nurse said: 'Aren't you going to ask me what it is?'

Michael and I looked at each other.

'What is it?' I enquired.

'Well, it's definitely a boy!' I must have looked

gobsmacked, and Michael was squeezing my hand so tight I thought he was going to cut off my circulation.

When we got outside, we both jumped up and down with excitement – which was quite impressive, considering how big I was at the time. Then we headed home, clutching the precious photos from the scan.

We decided Michael would move in with me, and soon afterwards, just before Christmas in fact, we sold my house and bought one together, complete with an extra room for a nursery.

On Christmas Eve, as I cuddled up to Michael, stroking my bump and admiring the gorgeous tree that had pride of place in our new sitting room in our new home, I had a flashback to a year earlier. Things had been so different then. I'd been standing in front of the mirror in my old house, wearing tight jeans and a spangly vest top, applying make-up and getting ready for a night on the razz with my girlfriends.

But so what if where I was now had been the last thing I'd expected? As far as I was concerned, Michael had proved himself ten times over by standing by me. I counted my blessings every day that I'd met such a lovely, reliable man.

So when, the following morning, Michael presented me with breakfast in bed – tea, croissants and a little blue Tiffany's box – he was greeted by happy sobs. Inside the box was a beautiful diamond engagement ring, and the minute I saw it all prior protests that he shouldn't feel the need to propose to me just because he'd got me 'up the duff' went out the window.

It was fantastic, and I actually felt really bad as, a couple of days earlier, I'd arranged to have my mum and Aunt Lorraine over for dinner. Michael had warned he might be a bit late home from work, but then turned up two hours later than he'd said. I was seething, telling him he'd embarrassed me in front of Mum, but now I realized why he'd been late – he'd driven all the way to London to pick up my ring from Tiffany's!

So, with my sparkly new ring on my finger, Michael and I spent Christmas morning enjoying a lazy lie-in.

When we finally surfaced and headed for my parents', I was met on the doorstep by a frantic-looking Mum.

'Did you say yes?' she spluttered. 'Oh, thank God for that. You're so late, I've been pacing up and down for an hour. I was worried you'd turned him down!'

It turned out that Michael had gone round the night before to ask my dad's permission to marry me.

Seven weeks later, our little boy arrived, well before he was supposed to make his entrance into the world.

We'd just returned home from a week in France, and my waters broke the following morning – five weeks early. Michael rushed me to hospital, the two of us poised for our son's arrival – but nothing happened. Instead, I spent an extremely boring week in hospital, watching with irritation as pregnant ladies came in and then left again with their bouncing bundles of joy.

I know it's not polite to glare at new mums but, honestly, I couldn't help it – how come they were all having babies and mine was stubbornly refusing to come? I was even starting to wonder if I could sneak a vindaloo into the maternity ward – by then, I was willing to try anything to help things along!

After seven days, just as I was losing the will to live, a doctor announced it was D-day. But after all that build-up, I can't actually tell you much about the birth. I think I was asleep for most of it.

It sounds bizarre, but I was terrified of hospitals so, before I went in, I'd been for some hypnotherapy, in the hope it would help to calm me down. Armed with all the techniques, when it came to the crunch, I was sort of able to hypnotize myself.

At the start, I remember them putting a needle in my hand, and that they kept missing the vein, which hurt, but as for the rest of my labour? I can't remember a thing.

The first thing I became aware of was an ominous cracking noise, which must have jolted me out of my hypnotic state. I remember telling Michael: 'I think I'm going to have the baby now!', then, with one almighty push, Jake was there, this long, thin baby.

There had been talk before his birth of having to put him in the special baby unit as a precautionary measure but, thankfully, despite being born so early, he was fine. He just looked like he'd grown to the right length, but hadn't bulked up.

As I held him in my arms and played with his tiny fingers and toes, he just seemed so perfect. In that instant,

I realized that I was actually very maternal after all. Who knew such a small thing could have such a huge impact on your life?

So, with our little bundle of joy safely delivered, there was just one thing left to make our little family complete, and that was our wedding day.

We'd already set the date for 1 March 2003 – a year and a day after Jake's birth – and we'd picked a gorgeous country house in Hampshire, so that it would be easy for Michael's family to get there from the south coast. Neither of us wanted a massive, grand wedding, so we settled on a small, intimate ceremony with about sixty guests.

Even with a small baby to care for, I really enjoyed the organizational side of things. I think I just have that gene which means I get a rush from ticking things off lists and filling folders with things done. With my compulsive need to organize, wedding planning was clearly the future career for me.

Not that it was plain sailing, of course. Planning a wedding is never easy, whether it's your own or someone else's, and the year leading from Jake's birth to the wedding was particularly hard, as my son had terrible colic and would constantly cry. In fact, as my mum correctly claims, for the first six months, all Jake did was 'scream, puke or sleep'.

I loved my baby, but being unable to settle him left me wired and on edge. Every day was an uphill struggle. I used to think to myself, 'If I can just cope with this until 6 p.m., then I can put him to bed.'

With Michael often away for work from Tuesday until Thursday, it was a lonely existence. Having Jake peacefully asleep in the evenings brought me relief, but also a feeling of isolation. The wedding gave me something to occupy my mind.

Most of the day, I'd feel like I had no control over my life; everything was dictated by Jake – when he needed to eat, be changed, be comforted. On more than one occasion, I'd venture out somewhere, only for him to scream blue murder. When people in the supermarket, who should really know better, gave me pointed looks, I'd ditch my plans to pick up any non-essentials and dash to the check-out.

'Don't stare at me!' I wanted to yell. 'I'm doing my best!'

At least, back in the sanctuary of my own home, the wedding was something I could influence and do a great job of. My desk was piled high with endless lists and spreadsheets – lists of things to do, lists for the guests and spreadsheets showing who'd replied and who wanted accommodation.

My guilty pleasure was sending away for samples of products or information packs. As sad as it sounds, when the postman rang the doorbell and handed over mystery parcels, it was just the fix I needed to brighten another day full of baby sick.

Being able to control the wedding and having people tell me I had everything 'so wonderfully planned' was a lifeline, reminding me that, perhaps, I could cope after all. When I was thinking about the wedding or doing things for it, I wasn't dealing with how depressed I was.

If I'd lost a lot of confidence through staying at home and, when I did go out, dodging the judgemental stares of people who thought I couldn't cope with my child, planning my wedding helped me to retrieve it. I had to call suppliers, I needed to go to various shops and talk to people. It kept me connected with life.

Ironically, after spending so much time in my childhood sketching dream wedding dresses, I didn't do a very good job of choosing my own.

Six weeks after Jake was born, I went dress shopping with Mum and my screaming, sickly child. I felt so lumpy and horrid trying on the dresses that, as soon as there was one that I didn't look like a complete train wreck in, I decided to go for it.

Choosing my wedding dress certainly wasn't the amazing experience I'd dreamed about, and when the dress came through, a month before the wedding, I had to take the bodice in by two sizes. Well, at least I'd lost my baby weight!

After that, whenever I felt low, I'd count down the days to the wedding, thinking about how wonderful it would all be. I'd wander over to my desk and check my lists. I could always find myself another job or task, and as my folders stacked up with neat notes and cuttings, I got a real feeling of satisfaction. I realized that, for me, wedding planning was completely addictive.

Michael, for the most part, was happy to let me take control. He was involved in choosing the venue, and the 'big things', like the photographer and the band, but I did all the research on suppliers before we went to see them and presented him with my lists on the nights he was home.

March crept nearer, and the week before our wedding I painstakingly packed everything I'd need to take to the venue: menus, place cards, the table plan, candles, gifts for our parents, my dress and shoes, jewellery, make-up. I was laden down – and, of course, had a list in my hand so I could check the items off as they went into the box. I had spares of everything, 'just in case'. I also planned to take my wedding folder with me on the day so I'd have all the details of the suppliers to hand should I need them. I had everything organized to the letter.

The only thing causing me stress was that Michael was having his stag do on the Thursday night, it was Jake's birthday on the Friday, and our wedding on the Saturday! I was worried he might be too ill to celebrate his son's first birthday at the special lunch party we were having for it. I ended up saying to him, 'I don't care what you do, so long as you don't end up puking on Jake's birthday.' (Apparently, he ended up in Stringfellows, but he stuck to his word, and didn't come home pissed, so I didn't care.)

Even though my wedding was meticulously planned, it didn't go without a glitch.

On the morning of our wedding day, I was hit by a bombshell: when I asked to see the co-ordinator at the venue, to whom I'd relayed all our plans for the previous six months, I was told she didn't work on Saturdays.

I was furious. When Michael and I first viewed the place,

it was she who had been the main selling point, the reason we'd picked it in the first place.

Although I'd done all the preparation myself, I'd trusted that, come the big day, she would be there, a safe pair of hands to make sure that everything unfolded just as I'd planned it. But no. Instead, the fate of our wedding lay in the hands of a banqueting manager we'd never met. It was kind of like going into labour and then realizing that the midwife you've had all the way through your pregnancy won't be the person delivering your baby.

The banqueting manager was a charming chap but, right from the beginning, there was a definite sense that the day was controlling him rather than the other way round. Consequently, I immediately got to work with Sarah, my 'best bird' as I called her, setting up the dining room. I knew exactly how I wanted the place settings to look, where the menus would go and where the favours would sit, and I didn't trust the venue to do it right. After all those evenings spent planning everything to the minutest detail, anything short of perfect just wasn't good enough.

Before the wedding, I'd begged the RAF to let me buy a certain type of ribbon, the same one that was used for one of the medals my late grandfather on my mum's side had won during the Second World War. I thought it would be a nice idea to use it as a wedding theme, as a way of dedicating the day to him, as he's a bit of a family hero. He was a pilot in the RAF, joining at the beginning of the war, and he flew in one of the first waves of planes that dropped parachutists behind German lines on D-day.

Grandad was also responsible for making landings to get the casualties out – and this bravery later won him the Air Force Cross.

On one occasion, he was on a mission when one of the parachutists got his line tangled underneath the plane. Grandad left the co-pilot in charge and then went to pull the guy back in. He saved his life. He died when I was four but, throughout my life, Mum, my gran and my great-aunts have told me so many amazing stories about him, he's always been an inspiration.

The ribbon from Grandad's medal was raspberry and ivory in colour, and I used the ribbon I had ordered to tie around the favours, the menus and the table napkins. Along the tables, I'd placed silver candelabras, and I also used the ribbon to wrap flowers around them. Then, around the edges of the room, I wanted big bay trees, with flowers and fairylights entwined in the branches.

Unfortunately, I was still faffing around making sure everything was ready at 2 p.m. – an hour before the ceremony was due to begin.

'Come on, Tam, it's time to leave,' Sarah instructed me, practically pushing me out of the room.

She was right: I had barely any time to slip into my dress and have my make-up done – not quite the relaxed preparation I'd planned. Thank goodness for my calm and unflappable friend, who helped me to wash and dry my hair, get showered, made up and photographed before heading down the aisle.

This was not shaping up to be the carefree day I'd

hoped for. The rosy glow I later sported as I walked down the aisle with my dad had nothing to do with the glass of champagne I'd managed to sneak in, but more to do with so far having spent the whole day dashing around like a lunatic.

I'd opted for a long, ivory, strapless dress, which I'd complemented with a tiara, to spruce up my short hair. I'd had it made specially so that it looked like RAF wings – again in honour of Grandad.

Michael and I had gone for a civil ceremony, in the same building as the reception, so at least I didn't have far to go. I just had to make my way out of my room and downstairs to a room that overlooked the gardens.

On the stroke of 3 p.m., Dad was outside my door, ready. I took a deep breath. Then, as Pachelbel's 'Canon in D' started, my bridesmaid, Michael's sister Donna, made her way into the room where Michael and I would take our vows.

After lots of deliberation, I'd decided that my bridesmaid should walk in first – mainly because, if she'd been behind me, she would have had to leap over my dress to get to her seat. (Later, when I'd embarked on my wedding-planning career, I suggested this to other couples. When the music starts, it can take a while for guests to shuffle around and stand up, and by the time they've got their cameras out, the bride can be halfway up the aisle. If you send the bridesmaids first, they can get to their seats easily, everyone else has stood up – and you build a nice sense of anticipation for the bride's entrance.)

So there I was at last, living the dream and walking down the aisle towards Michael, the man I loved and the father of my son. It was amazing.

The ceremony went like clockwork. Michael looked thrilled, and neither of us stuffed up our vows. All in all, it was pretty much perfect, and I spent the entire time grinning like a loon.

With our marriage sealed, it was time to celebrate, and all we had to do was walk from one room to another for our drinks reception. Hurrah!

As it was March and there was still a chill in the air, we'd decided to serve mulled wine and fruit juice. But when we walked into the room, I was dismayed to see that only the fruit juice had been laid out for our guests. The smile dropped from my face, and I immediately felt stressed. Where was the mulled wine? Surely the venue knew how long a civil ceremony would take? Surely they could have got things ready?

Instead of greeting our guests, I had to go and nag the staff to sort out the mulled wine; then, while they flapped around trying to organize it, I watched as everyone steamed in to snap up the juice.

Predictably, by the time the mulled wine finally appeared, there wasn't enough fruit juice left for those who didn't drink. It wasn't a catastrophe, but it mattered to me – especially as my mother is a non-drinker and was mingling with other guests without a drink in her hand.

'It's not a big deal,' I kept telling myself. 'Don't let it ruin your day.'

I was just beginning to enjoy myself again and was in the middle of a conversation with my cousin when someone next to me cleared their throat. It was our photographer.

'Sorry to bother you,' he said, 'but I was wondering if I could get access to one of the bedrooms so that I can take a group photo of everyone gathered outside from the window?'

So once again I had to break off from chatting to our guests and traipse off to ask for a key.

As the day wore on, there were loads of similar little incidents – for example, Sarah ended up lighting all the tea lights on the tables, because the staff hadn't done it; and the photographers weren't given their meals, even though we'd ordered and paid for them.

Although I was having a wonderful day, it did niggle at the back of my mind that all my careful planning was going out of the window.

But hiccups or not, I was thrilled with the enthusiastic reception the wedding was getting. People were having a great time, raving about the décor, and everyone was making a big fuss of Jake, who we'd dressed in a cute little pair of beige trousers, a white top and powder-blue sleeveless jumper. We'd arranged for there to be a high chair between Michael and my mum on the top table, and he just sat there looking at me with big eyes, clearly wondering what the hell Mummy was wearing.

We'd decided to have the speeches before the dinner. This way of doing things has since grown in popularity, and

I certainly went on to recommend it, as it means all the speakers can go on to relax and enjoy their dinner without knots in their stomachs from nerves.

Michael's speech was just lovely, and he got quite a few laughs from his audience, which is always a relief.

Next, my dad gave a brilliant speech, and at the end of it he and Mum presented me with a beautiful picture frame. Inside were all my grandad's war medals and, I have to say, I bawled my eyes out.

Once I'd composed myself, I decided to give an impromptu speech, thanking my friends and family and paying tribute to my new husband:

'As many of you know how dodgy Michael's timekeeping can be, the fact he turned up on time today is a pretty hopeful sign that he feels the same way about me as I do about him,' I told everyone. 'He is my biggest supporter, my best friend and now my husband – how fantastically lucky I am to get all that in one person.' I ended my speech by asking everyone to raise their glass to toast 'friends and family'.

Although the tradition is for the groom to make a speech, I'm pleased that more brides are now doing it as well. It's nice to be able to get up and thank the people who've helped you – particularly as the bride usually does the majority of the planning and so is the one who really knows who the unsung heroes are!

With the speeches over, everyone got stuck into their food, and later we cut the cake that Michael's mum had made for us.

The song we chose for our first dance was 'What a Wonderful World' by Louis Armstrong. Michael and I were no superstar dancers, so we went for something slow and relaxed. There's no point choosing anything difficult if you're worried about being on show. Just pick a short song with an obvious beat, then you can hang on to each other and just shuffle. As much as they'd like to see a *Strictly*-style foxtrot, all the guests really want to watch is the bride and groom having a cuddle and a kiss on the dancefloor.

Michael and I had one more special touch up our sleeves before the day was over. Instead of wedding gifts, we'd asked everyone to donate money to a charity called Canine Partners, which provides dogs for people with disabilities. Unbeknown to everyone, we'd invited Allen Parton, a representative of the charity, and his assistance dog Endal to the evening reception so that he could accept the cheque. He made an amazing speech, and everyone was crying.

A lot of couples make the mistake of having a magpie moment with their wedding list and subsequently end up with a load of tat that makes their home look like a poor man's Aladdin's cave. Picking out all the presents your heart could desire is exciting but, so often, when couples arrive at their department store of choice, they end up doing a bit of a frenzied supermarket sweep, and go round snapping up everything that is pretty and shiny.

Instead, the best thing to do is to sit together before the mad dash and write one list of things that you really want, and one of things it would be nice to have. Lots of stores now let you mark which items you'd most like to have on your list – so if you really want that KitchenAid food processor, you just might get it!

Of course, these days, many couples have already set up home with everything they could possibly need and, consequently, requests for gifts have become a bit more boring. Now people want John Lewis vouchers or cash donations towards their honeymoon, or even towards their DIY. Hardly inspiring, and not really very memorable.

You can still do something different and make it interesting, though. One couple I know put together a list of amazing things they wanted to do on their month-long honeymoon in Malaysia, so rather than simply depositing money into their bank account, the guests could tell the bride's sister that they wished to pay for a snorkelling trip, or whale watching, or moonlit meal on a cliff top overlooking the Indian Ocean. Each guest then received a commemorative photo of the couple enjoying their gift – much nicer.

I've even heard of one company that logs wedding guests' contributions against an account for house renovations, an interior designer or even a new conservatory. Or you can set up a gift list that will help you put together the wine cellar of your dreams, or even buy that amazing piece of art you both love.

While some people do find being presented with a wedding list a bit presumptuous on the part of the bride and groom and, equally, some couples are shy of offering one, if you don't tell people what you'd like then the chances are you'll have to prepare yourselves for an assortment of weird and wonderful artifacts from your nearest and dearest!

Wedding Gifts from Heaven and Hell

The Good . . .

'My most touching present was a surprise presented to me on the night by an old friend: a famous wine from the year we met.'

'A friend shot, edited and delivered to us by next morning a video, full of lovely messages and great footage of the entire day.'

'Knowing it had been my dream for a long time, my group of closest friends arranged for my new husband and I to swim with dolphins on our honeymoon.'

The Bad . . .

'My mother-in-law bought my husband a fire blanket! Hardly commemorative crystal, was it?'

'An aunt brought a home-baked cake to my wedding. Not my wedding cake. Just a cake. Five years on and I'm still baffled.'

'We got a wooden plaque with a heart suspended in the middle, painted with flowers and inscribed with a Bible quote – what on earth do you do with that? It was from an uncle, so I didn't have the heart to bin it (knowing him, it was probably blessed). It lives on the top of the dresser.'

The Ugly . . .

'His sister bought us a revolting eight-inch-tall "caricature" statuette of us both – and she told us the price!'

'My friend's German relatives presented them with a traditional wedding-themed candle that has to be the most phallic, hideous candle you have ever seen. It had a picture of the happy couple printed on to the front with glitter all around it and was like a huge, huge dildo.'

'I had a friend who was given a vibrator. For her wedding present? Why on earth?'

> 'In the wedding invitation the happy couple requested money — not for the honeymoon, or equipping their home, but towards the reversal of the groom's vasectomy.'

Whatever you receive, it's really important to have a plan in place to ensure that your presents do get to you.

I'll never forget the bride and groom who had all their wedding vouchers stolen from their reception venue. There was a little table for everyone to put their cards, next to one of the entrances to the hall. It was quite a large hotel, with people coming and going and, at some point in the evening, someone must have put their hand round the door and stolen all the envelopes.

When the bride called me the following day, she sounded so sad.

'I had such a lovely time,' she said, 'but now my final memory of my wedding day is when we realized everything had been stolen.'

Although her wedding insurance covered the vouchers, the fact that she'd lost the cards, with everyone's beautiful messages in them, was what grated the most.

The only way to avoid something like this happening is not to leave presents and cards out on display. Ask the venue to lock them away. (And that way, you can also avoid drunken guests falling into a stack of presents and breaking expensive china!) Another good tip is to make sure that your home insurance covers all your lovely new presents, so that you can head off on your honeymoon without worrying.

Having chosen to request donations to charity rather than gifts, at least that was one thing I didn't have to worry about at my wedding. Rather selfishly, I didn't throw my bouquet either; I saved it and, the next day, we placed it on Gran and Grandad's grave.

So that was that: my wedding day over far too soon. And after a fabulous honeymoon, staying at the Banyan Tree resort on Vabbinfaru in the Maldives, it was soon back to reality.

As many brides will testify, there can be a real sense of anticlimax once your wedding is over. You've spent all those months working up to this one big day. You've lived and breathed and devoted your life to it and then, in the space of a few hours, it's finished. You've packed away the dress, eaten the cake, opened the gifts and written the thank-you letters; the wedding is well and truly over, and it's back to the daily grind – and that's when post-nuptial depression can set in.

In the weeks after my wedding, I definitely had a bad case of PND. Planning the wedding had given me a purpose through those difficult months with Jake, and although he was now a much happier little boy and brought me so much joy, I could still feel myself slipping back into that old feeling of worthlessness.

It's not that being a mum wasn't fulfilling, far from it,

but when I'd tucked Jake safely into his cot each night, once again I was at a loss about what to do. As usual, Michael was away with work, and I was home alone with Jake.

I'd given up my marketing job when I went on maternity leave, and I didn't want to go back to it now. I saw it as quite a 'young' person's job, and although I was hardly a pensioner, being married with a child meant that I wasn't prepared to work regimented hours, and I certainly couldn't go to the pub after work every Friday like I used to. I felt the need to try something new, to throw myself into a new business venture in the way I'd attacked the preparation for my own wedding.

One evening, finding myself once again slumped miserably in front of the television, I realized that, for the sake of my sanity, I needed a job of some description – and not just a job but something I felt passionately about.

Often, in the evenings, I'd log on to the old wedding forums where I'd looked for ideas. With Jake asleep upstairs, it was nice to chat to other new brides. It stopped me from feeling quite so lonely. And it was as I sat at home one night chatting on a forum that an idea began to form in my mind.

As I swapped stories with these women about their weddings, we all seemed to have one thing in common – on our big day, we'd all had to rush off at some point to sort something out. These things seem so small and insignificant in hindsight but, at the time, after months of meticulous planning, the last thing you want on your wedding day is to be rushing around solving one mini-crisis after another. People's over-riding memory of the bride shouldn't be of the back of her dress as she hurries off to deal with another problem. After all that time, effort and money, it shouldn't be of another day of stress – it should be an absolute dream.

In my case, having planned everything so precisely, it made me realize how invaluable professional help would have been. The fact was, it didn't matter how much time and effort I'd put into everything in the run-up or how perfect it all looked on paper, it was all about being in control on the actual day. What I'd needed was someone else there to shoulder the burden.

I knew there were heaps of wedding planners out there, so it seemed silly to attempt to go into business in direct competition with established professionals.

But the more I thought about it, the more I realized that perhaps there was a market for an 'on-the-day' wedding-planning service, tailored specifically to couples who didn't want to fork out a fortune on someone to organize the whole thing.

At this point, I had no idea how to get to work on a wedding with a big budget, or with big, celebrity clients, and I assumed that brides with huge wads of cash to spend were relatively few and far between. But what if I started modestly, offering to deal with all the problems on the day in return for a reasonable fee?

My hunch was that loads of venue co-ordinators didn't work on Saturdays, so I started to phone around wedding venues.

'Does your wedding co-ordinator work on Saturdays?' I'd ask. 'Will she be there on the day for me?' I was amazed by how many said they didn't.

Finding out just before your wedding day that the person you've spent months planning the occasion with isn't going to be there is exasperating – yet it was clearly happening to so many couples all the time. Brides didn't know to check until it was the day itself, and by then it was too late to do anything about it.

Next, I did some research on wedding-planning companies to see if anyone was offering an on-the-day service. They weren't.

Taken as a whole, the wedding-planner industry was pretty snooty, with companies only taking on clients if they could pay massive fees to have everything done for them. I doubted any of these planners had worked with brides who were having their reception in their village hall, but surely these women needed help too?

The following week, as I sat sipping wine with one of my friends, I confided in her about my grand plan.

Debs, a down-to-earth Scottish girl who lived a few doors down from me, was always on hand to listen and, as one of the most caring people I knew, would definitely give me her honest opinion.

'I've just got a feeling I could be on to something,' I explained. 'I think there's a gap in the market I could capitalize on.'

'Yeah, you should go for it,' Deb agreed.

Over the next few days, an excited feeling washed over

me as my idea grew. Maybe I really could provide a service for couples who wanted to plan their own weddings but would be happy to pay to hand over all the responsibility and organization to someone else on the day itself? Surely there were hundreds of couples out there who could do with that kind of service?

I was a newlywed; I knew the market; I was very aware of the challenges of trying to do everything yourself on your wedding day. Plus, if I could just get this off the ground, I'd be running my own business from home, fitting work around family life and Jake.

So one night, about a month after the wedding, I mentioned it to Michael.

'I really think I could be on to something,' I told him.

'Well, why don't you give it a go?' he suggested. 'Just don't spend any money.'

So I started my business, TK on the Day, in May 2003, with just £100.

I liked the name: it wasn't too sickly-sweet like a lot of planner's names, TK being my initials and the 'on the day' bit neatly capturing the unique nature of the service – the idea that I would be there to co-ordinate the actual wedding, not take over the planning in the run-up. It definitely stood out.

I had a website built, which detailed the ethos of my company. I promised to run a couple's wedding day exactly as they'd planned it, and ensure that everything would happen at the right time and in the right way. Things would be in the correct place, and none of those oh-so-important little details would be forgotten. I would make sure they'd get everything they'd ordered or paid for, and I'd double check that any wine that hadn't been drunk with the meal was put behind the bar for later. Likewise, I'd take responsibility for hired items, ensuring they were all in place to be collected by suppliers the following day and that deposits were refunded. That way, the bride and groom could relax. I'd be there, in the background, ensuring that everything went smoothly.

I didn't want to risk forking out for advertizing at first, so I asked a few friends who were getting married in the near future to mention me on the wedding forums they frequented.

Word-of-mouth seemed to be the way forward. People immediately started emailing, and my phone didn't stop ringing. Within two weeks of announcing my new business, I'd picked up ten clients. It was crazy. People were booking me for late the following year, and for weddings in just a few months' time.

'I just want someone on my side,' one bride told me. She'd hit the nail on the head – the venue staff were employed by the venue, not by the bride. If she hired me, I'd be working for her.

As the work flooded in, it was a complete shock, as I hadn't really expected so much to happen so fast. If I'm honest, I was completely unprepared, and made a fair few mistakes before I started to get it right.

I got lost on my way to my first meeting with a client; when I launched my website my company brochures weren't ready; and I had to put together the information pack while trying to pacify a one-year-old toddling around my makeshift office. It was a baptism of fire, and I've since told wannabe planners I've trained to do the exact opposite.

It's not a job you should just fall into – so why, ten weeks after I dreamed up my plan, on the eve of my first wedding, was I lying in bed petrified at the thought of making a pig's ear of it?

2.
A Baptism of Fire

Terror, that's the only way I can describe it, utter terror. Here I was sorting out someone's big day, something they'd spent months planning, and if it all went wrong, it would be my fault. But there was nowhere to hide. I'd put myself up for this, so it was time to step up and take the wedding by the horns.

My very first clients were Barbara and Mitch and, to this day, I'm certain they had no idea how green I was.

The night before, I hardly slept a wink. By the time I'd finished printing off my notes, reading them for the hundredth time and packing a case full of things for emergencies, such as plasters, needle and thread, painkillers (for overzealous stags), spare ribbons, scissors, baby wipes and Rescue® Remedy, it was 2 a.m.

A painful four hours later, at the crack of dawn, I forced myself out of bed, butterflies in my stomach, and put on the wedding-planner attire I'd carefully selected.

Dressing for the part of a wedding planner had certainly been a conundrum. I didn't want to be 'office smart', as it wasn't a normal day at work, but I also didn't want to look like a guest when I wasn't one. Instead I wanted my outfit to be practical, neither too bright nor too sombre, and I needed to look professional and capable. Short skirts and low-cut tops were out.

After hours of deliberation and trying on practically everything in my wardrobe (where were Trinny and Susannah when you needed them?), I finally opted for a grey trouser suit with a black silk vest underneath and my favourite black Gina kitten heels.

All ready to go, I got into my little Alfa Romeo and set off on the twenty-mile journey from Basingstoke to Surrey, where the wedding was taking place, at Diane and Mike's house.

That weekend, the country was in the middle of a record-breaking heatwave, and by 8 a.m., when I arrived, it was already baking.

Having promised to set everything up for them, I was immediately thrown in at the deep end.

Marquee weddings are really hard work, as you pretty much have to do it all. When you get there, all you have is the floor down and the tables in position, and from that you have to assemble everything. Sometimes the waiting staff will help, but I was very much on my own that day.

Already sweating in the heat, I laid out the tablecloths and set to work arranging all the decorations, place settings and favours.

When I'd finished, I stood back and took in the scene. It looked great, even if I do say so myself. I think the closet girlie girl in me secretly loved making everything pretty, even if I was constantly watching the clock.

The marquee had been designed to fit the space in Diane and Mike's garden perfectly, and with a stunning candlelit canopy and flowers from the garden, it looked lovely. There were also lights strung around the house's verandas and garden, and flares to be lit up at nightfall. It was going to look amazing.

Yet I was sick with nerves at the thought of what the day would entail. There were so many small details that could go wrong – I was even more nervous than I'd been at my own wedding.

One of the things I'd offered to do for the bride and groom was to announce their arrival into dinner, and the thought of it was already making me shake. 'What the hell am I doing?' I muttered to myself.

But I soon discovered there were more pressing problems at hand.

The temperature was soaring, and even without anyone in the marquee, the heat was seeping through the canvas walls and creating a greenhouse effect. Add a big group of revellers into the mix, and it was going to get a lot hotter in there.

Sweaty guests are never a good look, and a perspiring bride should never be seen. Yet even before the service, poor Diane had kitchen roll tucked into the top of her dress because she was perspiring so badly and in danger of staining her gown.

'Can I have a word?' I asked Diane's dad, Ed, before they set off to the church. 'I'm worried about the marquee,' I explained, pointing to the already wilting flowers. 'It's like a sauna. I was thinking of driving into town to see if I could pick up some portable air-conditioning units.'

'That's a really good idea,' he replied. 'If you do that, we'll roll up the sides of the marquee to try and get some air flowing through.'

So I rushed into town and found an electrical store, and picked up two air-conditioning units. By the time the newlyweds returned, jubilant after their wedding service at the local church, I'd fixed the units up in the tent and had managed to lower the temperature a little. It was still roasting, but there was definitely a marked improvement. Yay!

After the guests had had drinks in the garden, I was informed by the caterers that the time had come – I had to find my voice and call everyone into dinner. My stomach lurched at the thought and, taking a deep breath, I gave myself a silent pep talk. 'They don't know you've never done this before,' I told myself. 'Just act confident, and they'll believe in you.' So, clearing my throat, I did just that.

I don't know what I was expecting – heckles, or funny looks, at the very least – but it was completely fine. I've learned since that the majority of guests are quite happy to switch off and just follow someone else's instructions. It's when people are left waiting without knowing what's going on that problems start.

Feeling almost as proud as Barack Obama must have done after pulling off his first presidential speech, I buzzed around, keeping a close eye on the caterers. But before long I was faced with my next problem – a deaf guest with a cut hand. I managed to communicate with him, though, and bandage him up. Aha, I knew those plasters would come in handy!

All around me, people were getting quite drunk – going through the wine and the water with even more gusto than usual, due to the heat. Drinking so much also meant more trips to the loo, and when I checked, it appeared that the toilet-roll reserves were getting very low. I jumped back in my car and headed for the nearest supermarket to stock up on bottles of water and toilet paper.

As I wheeled out a trolley stacked full of bottled water and bog roll and battled to fit it all in the limited space in my car boot, I had my first indication that wedding planning was not actually that glamorous. Somehow I couldn't imagine J-Lo staggering across a car park up to her ears in Andrex Warm Natural, but it was all worth it to see Diane and Mike looking relaxed and happy, seemingly unconcerned with any problems or dramas, the way they should be on their wedding day.

I was thrilled when they even asked if they could have a picture taken with me. It was really nice that they were appreciative. I was definitely off to a good start – and I was hooked from then on.

Throughout my career as a wedding planner, I was constantly learning on the job, and I certainly had two valuable lessons that day.

The first was at about 4 p.m. – that, pretty as my silly little Ginas looked, I might as well have welded hot irons to the bottom of my feet for the agony they caused.

The second really hit home at 2 a.m., as I finally left the marquee, limping and barely able to keep my eyelids open: offering to stay until the last guest went home was an unnecessary sacrifice on my part. Some people really can't tell when a party's over and just have to be the last man standing – plus, once the boogieing begins, there is very little for the wedding planner to do.

That first wedding was the longest and most physically painful day of my life. When the last guest finally lurched out of the marquee clutching a bottle of whiskey, it took all the determination I could muster just to stagger to my car.

After taking my shoes off and looking at my poor, burning, bruised feet, I discovered that they were so swollen I couldn't actually change gear. I had to drive home all the way in third gear, wincing and with my eyes watering from the pain.

The following morning, as I lay on the sofa completely exhausted and with a packet of frozen peas on my feet, I couldn't help but smile. Despite the heat, chaos and dramas, it had been worth it. I'd had a really good day and felt really proud of myself. I'd coped with everything that was thrown at me, and no one was any the wiser to just how new to the business I was. My feet might have been throbbing like I'd just run a marathon on hot coals, but I'd done it. I'd pulled off the on-the-day organization of a whole wedding and given the bride and groom a really good service to boot.

It seemed Diane and Mike thought so too. The next

day, to my delight, I received an email from Diane saying how pleased she'd been with the way the day had gone. I was so chuffed I almost printed it out and framed it!

After that, I was off and rolling – there would be no stopping me now. I just hoped my next jobs would go as smoothly.

Over the next few weddings, my feet now comfortably encased in sensible, flat shoes, I began to learn more lessons on the hop.

Although I'd originally charged just £250 for the whole day, the work involved soon hit home, and I put it up to £350 for a set period from three hours before the ceremony until the last dance. People could then add extra hours if they wanted, for an additional cost.

I also set myself a rule to always be cool. I'd never run or dash around the wedding, as that would alarm the bride and make her think something was wrong. Nobody wants to see a red-faced woman fleeing from one room to the next.

My second rule was to answer every question with the phrase: 'It'll be fine.'

Thirdly, lecherous best men and fathers were to be avoided at all costs.

It was just one month into my wedding-planning career that I got groped by a guest. I was leaning over the bar asking the staff if everything was going to plan when I felt a hand squeeze my backside.

Turning around, I looked quizzically at the owner of the over-friendly mitts.

'Ah, Tamryn,' the father of the groom, who was clearly quite well oiled, boomed. 'What a wonderful job you're doing!'

His smile spread from ear to ear, and he didn't seem the least bit embarrassed.

'Thanks, that's very kind,' I managed to muster before making my excuses and heading off.

A while later, I bumped into him in the hotel reception. He was now even drunker, swaying slightly and clutching a bottle of champagne and two flutes. He stepped closer to me and moved his head so that whatever he had to say would be out of earshot of the other guests.

'How about we go upstairs to my room with this,' he growled, indicating the bottle. 'I'd love to show you my appreciation!'

As I stood there contemplating how on earth you respond to an offer like that, and slightly alarmed by his lechy grin, my knight in shining armour came, courtesy of the head of catering.

'Is it okay if I steal you away for a word?' he said.

'Yes!' I nearly shrieked, nodding emphatically as he asked if it was all right for his staff to head off.

I spent the rest of the evening doing my best to avoid my portly admirer, and a while later I was relieved to spy him in a corner chatting up a rather uncomfortable-looking bridesmaid.

'You've done such a wonderful job today,' I heard him slurring, as she stood there like a rabbit caught in the headlights.

Poor girl, was all I could think. Rather her than me, though!

I don't know what it is about weddings, but I've never been propositioned so much in my life. Suddenly, dirty old uncles were sauntering up to pinch my bum and best men were trying to manhandle me on to the dancefloor during the smoochy songs.

At first, I probably tolerated it more than I should have. I gritted my teeth and smiled sweetly, not wanting to cause a scene or upset the happy couple. But then I began to recognize the signs.

When people are drunk, they are not subtle, so if I spotted the old family friend eyeballing me continually and then heading over, I'd simply wander off in a different direction.

I also learned the wonder of selective deafness. Lecherous comments and pawing advances could be cut dead with a simple comment such as, 'Oh, I must just go and see to those flowers . . .'

The worst sleazer I experienced was actually a groom, believe it or not.

Greg wasn't your usual loved-up husband-to-be, and I took a dislike to him pretty much from the moment I met him. He was just one of those lecherous types who doesn't even try to disguise the fact that they're checking you out.

'So this is the gorgeous Tamryn!' he remarked, stepping through the door.

His bride-to-be, Ellie, giggled in response, strangely

oblivious to the fact that his eyes were fixed firmly on my breasts. Nice.

All I could think was, 'Gosh, you've done well for yourself, haven't you?'

There was no doubt that, in the looks and personality department, Greg was punching well above his weight with Ellie, who had that enchanting combination of beauty and loveliness. I tried to give him the benefit of the doubt, but throughout our meetings he was always a bit too friendly for my liking. He'd touch me on the arm when it wasn't necessary and loom in to kiss me with a look of glee on his face at the start of each meeting.

But it was on the day of the wedding that Greg really excelled himself. We were all set to go, with Greg and his best man ready to position themselves at the front of the church, when he turned to me with his textbook sleazy smile. Looking me up and down, he leaned in close to my face, his mouth almost brushing my cheek. 'Such a shame it's not you at the end of the aisle, Tamryn,' he whispered, his hand squeezing my waist.

I was completely aghast. 'Yeah and hell would freeze over first . . .' I raged in my head. Then I put on my best poker face and took a step backwards.

'Right,' I announced in an efficient tone. 'I'll just see if your *beautiful bride* has arrived yet.' Then I turned on my heels, fighting the urge to beg Ellie to reconsider marrying such a revolting, slimy dirtball.

For someone who's never had men falling at her feet, all these incidents were a bit strange. Was it a 'woman in authority' thing, or just beer goggles? Thank God groping groom Greg was a one-off.

As I met couple after couple who wanted me to plan their wedding, the good feeling and happiness that radiated from them was contagious. No matter what sort of day I was enduring, having two people sit in front of me, holding hands and sharing sweet little sideways smiles, immediately took me back to the heady high I'd experienced as a twelve-year-old watching love (albeit make-believe) blossom between my favourite soap characters, Scott and Charlene. I had high hopes of a 'happy ever after' for these couples too, and it was a lovely experience to help them on their way.

As month after month went by, I learned even more on the job, filling my folders with essential notes and tips for wedding planning. I might only be helping on the day, but as each wedding presented different issues and dilemmas, I got a real insight into all the things that can go wrong if couples don't ask the right questions, and I passed this on to my clients in the hope it would help them in the lead-up to their big day.

One of the biggest traps spouses-to-be seemed to fall into in the run-up to their wedding was rushing to book their venue without fully investigating what the hidden costs would be. Once you've paid the deposit, it's a big commitment, so you're much better off putting in the time to find the right venue, and if you do decide to sign up with somewhere, it's wise to study all the extra lines tucked away that might have information about additional charges.

One couple who asked me to cover their wedding had been stung by a venue that would charge them a fortune if they didn't book out every room for overnight accommodation. There were extra fees for bringing in suppliers not recommended by the venue, and the cost went up if the wedding guests numbered over seventy-five so the venue could cover their costs for bringing in more staff.

There was also something in the small print about a 10 per cent increase in prices each year, on 1 January, so this lovely couple were, strangely, being penalized for booking their wedding in advance. Sneaky fee increases are also often added if you want the bar to stay open later, a dancefloor put down or if you want to get into your bridal suite before 12 p.m. to get ready.

And it isn't just the venues that try it on; there are also plenty of suppliers out there who don't show the 'extras' in their package prices. All of a sudden, the band or photographer who was just within your budget becomes much more expensive once you've added in mileage costs, food, and even overnight accommodation for them. While the majority of suppliers are honest and upfront, there are a small minority who are not as candid, so you should always ask before signing your life away. One poor bride of mine, Hatty, had absolutely no faith in her venue delivering the wedding of her dreams. Over the six months since she'd booked her wedding, she'd been introduced to no fewer than four in-house wedding co-ordinators, and each one was younger and less experienced than the one before. Let's be honest, would you want the work-experience girl running your big day?

The final straw was not when she was sent an email in which they got her wedding date wrong but the day when she made an appointment to go to the venue to show her mum, only to get there and for them to deny all knowledge of her.

When I met her she was a nervous wreck, so we went through all of the details for the day and I prepped her on the information she needed to give to the venue. I told her to ask to be sent a copy of the venue's notes for her day so that she could check everything. Well, lo and behold, when the email arrived, the attached information sheet was for a completely different wedding. I was beginning to understand why she thought the staff at the venue were totally incompetent. But, together, we made sure they had all the right information and battled on with it.

The day itself was an interesting experience for me, as it was clear that lots of the staff were very enthusiastic but hadn't really had any training. On top of that, the managers didn't seem to understand why it was all so important to the bride. In their eyes, it was just another corporate day, where as long as they kept the alcohol flowing no one would care about anything else, which is completely the wrong attitude.

As it turned out, Hatty finally did get the day she deserved, and as she glided around, looking radiant in her fitted bodice and layered American tulle skirt, I knew that all the problems she'd endured were now long forgotten.

How to Avoid the Venue Pitfalls

DON'T take anything as read without checking first. The venue might not allow fireworks or candles, for example, and don't assume that you can stay there after midnight. You have to ask lots of questions.

DO ask if there is going to be another wedding on the same day. There is nothing worse than bumping into another bride in the toilets. You don't want to know that there are loads of other people at the venue doing the same thing. Every bride wants to think it is her special day.

DON'T fall into the trap of thinking everything will be perfect. I once planned a wedding for a couple whose requirements were very specific: their wedding had to be at a venue by water with mountains in the background. But then, when we found it, they didn't like the colour of the carpet. There's no point getting hung up on the little things if all your other boxes are ticked. If you don't like the carpet colour, then you can use decorations to direct people's eyes away from it. If you start to fall into the trap of never being satisfied, then it's bound to be awful.

DO think: quality, not quantity. If you cram in

loads of things – candles, lights, flowers, favours, table confetti, table cameras and all the other wedding-related 'essentials' – then your guests won't notice anything. It'll all look too muddled. Let people notice things.

DO make sure you find a decent wedding snapper. In years to come, when your wedding is nothing but a faint memory, it is your photos that will immediately put you back in the moment.

You have to pity the couple who made national headlines when they took their photographer to court for breach of contract after he returned appalling photos of their big day – including one with their heads chopped off. The range of snaps apparently featured out-of-focus shots, random close-ups of cars, guests looking bored and, to add insult to injury, a naked photo of a three-year-old bridesmaid, which the photographer then refused to remove from his website, despite repeated requests. A video recording of the church ceremony also featured a scene where the operator dropped his equipment and swore. Add to this the fact that there were no pictures of the newlyweds arriving at their reception or cutting the cake, and you can really sympathize.

Not surprisingly, a judge found in favour of the angry newlyweds, ordering the photographer to pay back £500 of the £1,450 they'd paid to him. It was no doubt a hollow victory for the couple, who are left with mediocre photographs of what should have been the best day of their lives. They certainly didn't get to enjoy the buzz of seeing their photos and then showing them to friends and family.

I'm pleased to report that the majority of photographers are really good at their jobs, but it is stories like this that highlight just why you should err on the side of caution when it comes to booking a snapper. Rely on word-of-mouth and testimonials, and check portfolios that illustrate their style.

I can remember one wedding and being there on the day that the mother of the bride had booked the photographer. When I asked her the name of his company, I'd never heard of him.

'How did you find him?' I asked tentatively.

'I found him online. He had a great website!' she replied proudly. 'And when you book him, you get ten free disposable cameras!'

At that point, alarm bells really began to ring. If that was his selling point, then it was definitely not good news.

As I suspected, he wasn't up to the job.

When he arrived, he turned out to be a slightly older guy with slicked-back hair that made his bald spot all the more noticeable, and he was wearing a leather jacket, grey shirt and trousers, and a smile that made me immediately think 'weasel'. I clocked straight away that he had no spare camera, no extra gear and no assistant. Not an encouraging sign.

Pretty early on, I caught him taking a photo of the bride and her beloved grandmother with a refrigerated lorry in the background. He clearly had zero initiative, so from then on I had to follow him around constantly, pointing out good photo opportunities or suggesting that perhaps positioning the bridesmaids in front of a lamppost wasn't the best idea. I hoped that, with my intervention, the photos could just about be saved although, sadly, they weren't going to be good, by any stretch of the imagination.

Sure enough, some while after the wedding, I had an email from the bride asking what I'd thought of the photographer. Apparently it had taken four months to get the proofs of the photos through, and when they did get the album, the photographer had spelled the groom's name wrong. Not good.

It's absolutely essential that, when you meet a photographer, you ask to see at least three or four complete albums – not just a few random highlights from a lot of weddings but all the shots from a wedding. If you can see that the selection is consistently good and the style suits you, you're on the right track.

Make sure you like the way they handle the shots from both the ceremony and the reception. Also, check out the group shots. Do they all have the same background? Has the photographer just positioned the bride and groom and swapped other guests in and out, or have they shown some creativity and variation and moved everyone around a bit?

A trend in recent years is for disposable cameras to be placed on tables for guests to have fun with. In my experience, this can be a bit hit and miss. Normally, when you get the photos back, you'll have at least fifteen pictures of the best man making his speech and the bride and the groom cutting the cake – or if a child has got hold of the camera, there may be lots of close-ups of shoes and the carpet.

I've definitely had quite a few cases where couples have got back the pictures taken by disposables only to discover lots of photos of bottoms. And on one occasion a bride was very amused to find snaps of all her friends from university sliding down the banisters in a stately home.

Six months after I launched TK on the Day, I was faced with my first clash of dates. A couple wanted me to take on their wedding, but they were getting married on a day when I'd already committed to someone else. It pained me to turn down work, so I decided that perhaps now was the time to think about getting some help. Perhaps I could find some women who I could train up as wedding planners?

I put an advert on my website and, immediately, CVs started to flood in. Two girls stood out – Liz and Sarah – so I arranged to interview them. They both impressed me, so I hired them straight away.

Bev, a blonde, friendly-looking girl, was from Buckinghamshire and very young. But she absolutely loved weddings and really sold herself to me during her interview. The brides loved her. Chloe was from Kent, and was dark with a huge smile. She was planning her own wedding when she started working with me, so the extra money was handy and she really empathized with the brides. I figured that the fact they were from different areas was useful as it would mean that TK on the Day would be able to cover more ground.

Before they looked after any weddings, I went through with them both the principles of the business and the service I was providing. Then I asked them to accompany me on a training day, where they shadowed me at a wedding.

Once they were fully trained, Bev and Chloe took home the whole fee for covering the wedding, the pre-wedding meetings and email support with the client, minus £150 commission, which I ploughed back into the business.

One of the things we'd do at the pre-wedding meetings was to ask the couples to unburden themselves of any worries. Well aware of how these little worries can eat into a couple's enjoyment of their day, before every wedding I'd take them through a questionnaire I'd compiled, asking them to tell me about any concerns.

'What's your biggest worry?' I'd ask. 'What can we do to avoid it?'

Then, instead of burying their heads in the sand and hoping and praying that an issue wouldn't arise, we could work on a contingency plan that would spring into action should their worst-case scenario actually occur.

It might be nerves about being the centre of attention, or concerns about a dress not fitting, but nothing gets people's pulses racing like the F-word – family. You love them, you hate them and, more often than not, some of them hate each other too. It's not exactly a recipe for a calm and peaceful day.

Quite early on in my wedding-planning career, I found out how divorces, falling-outs and politics within families can be a logistical nightmare for the bride and groom, who just want to celebrate their big day with people they love.

Take Belinda, whose fiancé and father fell out three weeks before the wedding and so weren't talking to each other on the day. To make matters worse, Belinda hadn't had a lot of contact with some of her mother's family, so only invited a couple of her mother's siblings to her big day – a decision that was met with outrage.

'After the wedding I found out that the excluded branch of the family had told the "chosen ones" that if they went to my wedding they would be made outcasts,' she revealed. 'It was all very *EastEnders*, but they chose me and there was a huge family rift! We're all just about speaking to each other again.'

It sounds extreme, but family divisions at weddings are actually a really common issue. So if you're in this situation, take heart, because you are definitely not alone. These days, all kinds of difficult factors come into play. Maybe parents have got divorced and want to bring their new partners, or perhaps meddling family members don't approve of the bride's choice of husband. If you want to see how quickly the temperature can drop on a stunning summer's day, just put a divorced mother and father of the bride together at the top table – icy stares all round.

There's so much emotion surrounding weddings that it's

not uncommon for people to use them as an opportunity to put someone in their place, or even not to invite them to 'teach them a lesson'. Yes, there's nothing like a wedding to bring out your inner teenager and make everyone feel like they're back in the school playground.

But the decisions you are making take on so much importance. You can never go back and change things if you made the choice not to invite, for example, your stepmother. You will never be able, in the future, to undo that slight and the insult and hurt it may have caused.

The good news is that most family tensions can easily be avoided.

With the worst possible timing, at one wedding we were faced with the dilemma that the bride's parents had decided to go their separate ways just a week beforehand. Awkward, to say the least, but with no one except the immediate family in on the secret, the gossip was kept at bay.

Keen to maintain things as low key as possible, the bride and I worked out an emergency plan to ensure that her parents weren't standing next to each other for the photos, and we also had a little play with the table plan. It worked a treat, and nobody suspected a thing.

If you think that you have to stick to the regimented formality of traditional wedding etiquette, then think again! If it doesn't work for you, then no one's going to mind if you adjust it accordingly – just like I did with the speeches on my wedding day.

You don't have to do things by the book. There is always scope for adapting the rules to suit your personal situation as a couple. So, for example, if you don't have a good relationship with your dad then ask your mum to make a speech. There is no need to follow etiquette if it just isn't going to work that way.

The third wedding I covered was for a couple called Lara and David, who decided to tackle the feud in their family by simply not tolerating huffy looks and snide comments on the top table.

It was clear when we discussed the politics that there wasn't a hope in hell of everyone being seated together and playing happy families over salmon and champagne. So instead it was decided that Lara and David would have a special top table for two in between tables seating the rest of the bridal party. It was the perfect set-up, as they were close to everyone yet also managed to grab some time to talk without anyone having a huge fall-out or throwing daggers across the main course – a wise decision, not least because Lara and David were cutting their cake with an army sword belonging to one of their guests. The thought of that being waved around was already giving me nightmares, without adding disgruntled family members into the mix.

It's amazing what problems you can avoid if you take the time to look out for things that might go wrong. If there's a risk of people making trouble, then a well-timed word from the best man that 'This is someone's wedding' might be all it takes to restore calm.

At problematic weddings, I learned to make a point of singling out the known troublemakers and would attempt to build a relationship with them early on. That way, when they were a few beers along the line, I could ask them to calm down and the likelihood was that they'd listen.

Of course, it's not always quite so easy to solve a family feud, especially when it's been around for a long, long time. However, despite being a hotbed for potential drama, a wedding can actually be a great opportunity to heal rifts and start again. By extending your hand and making an effort to invite someone you've previously fallen out with, all sorts of quarrels and upset can be cast aside.

I remember one groom who'd fallen out with his brother when their parents had divorced. Jake had sided with his mother, while his older brother, Nick, had supported his dad. As a consequence, the two siblings hadn't spoken in six years.

Although Jake was adamant that he didn't need to invite Nick or his father, his bride, Lucie, was concerned that, in years ahead, he might regret it.

'If you leave them out, they'll always remember it,' she told him. 'At least invite them, and it will give you the chance to make up. I don't want you to have any regrets.'

Jake's father declined the invitation, but Nick accepted.

Although, when Nick first arrived, things were a little frosty between the two brothers, over the course of the day, they both began to thaw. And by the end of the evening, I was thrilled to see them propping up the bar together having a drink.

As I watched them, Lucie came bounding towards me with a wide smile.

'Thank God for that,' she said. 'I've been so worried. I've had sleepless nights, thinking it will be all my fault if they have a massive bust-up!'

She needn't have worried. After that, Jake and Nick started to see a lot more of each other, and there was even talk of Jake meeting up with his dad. So, no matter how bad things seem, there's always the hope of reconciliation.

I can remember another wedding where the groom's friends were ridiculously snobby because they believed him to be marrying below his station.

Charlie had met his bride at university, but his close-knit circle of friends, who'd all gone to the same prestigious public school, were less than impressed.

Charlie, who had lords and ladies in his family, had come from 'good stock', they believed, unlike cabbie's daughter Simone, who came from a working-class area in the North – and you thought Kate Middleton had it tough!

Apparently, they'd even taken him aside on the stag do and expressed concern that she was 'after his money'. For people who clearly considered themselves to be impeccably well bred, I personally thought that showed very little class.

But Charlie, to his credit, knew his own mind and wisely kept his friends' nasty comments from Simone. Instead, he quietly instructed them to put a sock in it or not bother coming at all. So the la-di-da brigade turned up – if only to sneer at the natives from 'oop North'.

When Simone's mum arrived on the day clutching an Iceland carrier bag, I did cringe for her. I could actually see Charlie's friends' noses crinkling in disgust.

'Good God, it's like an episode of *Shameless*,' I heard one posh girl exclaim with nasal distaste.

'Oh Lord, how is this all going to pan out?' I wondered to myself.

But then, as the booze began to flow after the ceremony, the guests started to mingle. Although, to start off with, there was a clear divide on the dancefloor – like the Jets and the Sharks in *West Side Story* – after a while, they all began to shake their stuff. Then, in an act of sheer brilliance, a member of Simone's family requested the 'Macarena'. Suddenly, an uncle in Charlie's family, who was a lord, could be seen dancing next to Simone's cousin, who was teaching him every hip-thrusting and arm-flailing move with gusto. By the end of the night, everyone was getting on like a house on fire, and all trace of any class divide had been forgotten. Afterwards, I heard, Charlie even got an apology from his toff pals, and at last Simone was accepted into the inner circle.

At the other end of the scale, you have family and friends who couldn't get on better – like those of Claire and Alex.

On the day of their wedding, a very special surprise was secretly arranged to showcase this during the father of the bride's speech. Before the wedding I'd helped Claire's dad rig up a large screen behind a curtain, which was going to be whipped away at the crucial moment. The two sets of parents had put together a ten-minute film in the style of *This is Your Life*. It had been an ongoing exercise to try and keep it a secret, but it was worth every ounce of trouble.

When the film rolled, the guests were treated to funny and cute pictures of Claire and Alex growing up, segued with memories and stories from family members. It ended with all four parents together toasting the couple with champagne. Claire and Alex were both completely gob-smacked, and very touched.

It's moments like those that will stick with couples for so many years afterwards, when all thoughts of the cake, the wedding favours and what colour the flowers were have faded to nothing.

As I ticked off each wedding and carefully made notes on lessons learned and what had and hadn't worked, I really began to realize just how high emotions can run – and not just for the newlyweds. Maybe it's a combination of the rivers of alcohol and the sentiment of the day, but weddings are a hotbed for people getting together – or, unfortunately, splitting up.

On one occasion, I watched as, tragically, a bridesmaid and an usher called time on their relationship just as their best friends were committing to a lifetime together.

To be honest, it had been clear from the off that some-thing was going on as, during the wedding rehearsal, the bridesmaid had been unsubtly snippy with her boyfriend.

While the bride and groom were getting excited, 'Snide' and 'Gloom' were clearly getting on each other's nerves.

'You've been told to stand over there,' I heard the brides-maid snap when her usher boyfriend had failed to position himself in exactly the right spot, and the poisoned arrows

68

continued to be fired as they practised their roles in the church.

I'd hoped that they'd sort out their differences overnight, but on the day of the wedding they were again at each other's throats. She wouldn't stand next to him for photos, and even moved the place cards on the table so that they weren't seated next to each other. Something was clearly going to kick off.

Lo and behold, after they'd both sunk a skinful of champagne, their resentment towards one another finally came to a head. Embarrassingly, the resulting screaming match took place on the terrace, in front of several guests. The usher, to his credit, tried to get her to go somewhere more private, but by that point she was hysterical.

'I don't want to move,' she yelled. 'I'm so better off without you, I don't want to see you after today.'

Of course, the bride and groom got wind of it, and the bride, being kind-hearted, spent half the evening in the toilet trying to comfort her friend.

For every couple who break up mid-wedding, though, there are several who see love blossom as they playfully clink champagne glasses and smooch around on the dancefloor to Barry White.

Take best man Colin, who wowed wedding guest Anne, as he turned white with fear in the lead-up to his speech.

Anne claims that her first impression of Colin was to marvel at his ghostly-pale complexion. It would make *Twilight* hunk Edward Cullen look positively rosy-cheeked.

'I just feel so nervous,' he confided to Anne, within

minutes of being introduced. Despite the fact that Colin looked on the verge of regurgitating his breakfast, Anne decided that his honesty was refreshingly endearing.

Later, Colin admitted that his initial over-riding impression of Anne was that she looked like a bumblebee in her yellow mini dress and huge sunglasses – but he liked it.

The lovers-to-be didn't actually speak again properly until around 2 a.m., by which time Colin's speech had gone down a storm and he had plenty of colour back in his cheeks.

As the night descended into debauchery, Anne spilled a bottle of red wine all over a group of Colin's friends and, having almost caught up with her on the drinks front, Colin was filled with Dutch courage. When Anne's friends told him to walk her back to the stately home where everyone was staying, he duly used it as an opportunity to go in for a kiss. Anne was only too happy to oblige, and they ended up spending the night together.

Indeed, things were going so well that Colin was still in Anne's bed the next morning, when he was meant to be at a Team Bride *vs* Team Groom football match. Oops. Team Groom was banging on his hotel door, 'incandescent with rage', as they put it – not that he was bothered. Meanwhile, Anne had most definitely scored. A year later, Colin proposed, and they are now happily married. Awww. There's plainly nothing like a wedding to get everyone in the mood for lurrrve.

In another love story that could have been plucked from

Four Weddings and a Funeral, I recall smiling to myself as a spark began to ignite between an usher and a bridesmaid as they sat outside sharing a bottle of wine. Clearly besotted, they were inseparable for the rest of the day, and I even spotted them having a smooch and a little kiss on the dancefloor. Being a wedding planner is sometimes like being a fly on the wall – you get to see everything without being noticed.

I didn't really think any more about this little romance until six months later, when I received an email from the bride telling me that the young couple in question were still together – and now planning their own wedding. Ain't love grand?

And wedding-related romances aren't just for the youngsters. It's amazing how the feel-good factor of a wedding can have a magnetic effect on everyone involved – young and old.

In another touching scenario, I witnessed how a bride's divorced parents found love again as they helped plan their daughter's nuptials.

Before my first meeting with Kerry, the bride, she'd called to warn me of the situation with her parents.

'They're both coming to the meeting,' she explained, 'but it won't be a problem.'

I'd envisaged some kind of tension, but it was quite the opposite. There wasn't a hint of bad feeling between Maureen and Alan – in fact, they seemed to get on like a house on fire.

'Maybe you could keep the top tier of the cake for when

you have a baby, like we did at our wedding,' Maureen suggested as the meeting went on.

'That's a great idea,' Alan chirped in response, while everyone grinned in agreement.

It was like a bloody episode of *The Waltons* – but I really quite liked it.

Another six months down the line, Kerry called to say that the wedding preparations were going swimmingly.

'Mum and Dad are getting on sooo well,' she added, a hint of scandal in her voice. 'They went out to dinner to talk about the plans last week. I've got a real feeling they might get back together!'

Well, it turned out her intuition was right. A month before the wedding, Mum and Dad gathered the family together for a 'big announcement'.

'They're trying again!' Kerry shrieked down the phone to me.

At the next meeting when we did a last-minute run-through of all the plans for the day, Kerry and Nick certainly had some stiff competition for soppy, lovelorn looks. There were Maureen and Alan, holding hands and grinning from ear to ear.

'We've had such a nice time organizing the wedding,' Maureen confided. 'It's reminded us of why we fell in love in the first place.' How lovely.

On the day of the wedding, when Maureen and Alan strolled into the church arm in arm, there were knowing smiles all round. You could tell that everyone knew and was really happy about it, but they weren't out to upstage Kerry and Nick on their day. In any case, I don't think the bride or groom could have asked for a nicer present.

By now I was nine months into my wedding-planning career and starting to make money. I hadn't spent much starting up, and my overheads were small, so almost from the word go the money I made was profit.

It would still be some time before the money really started rolling in, but I'd had full payments on the weddings I'd already done and deposits for the ones that were coming up. I knew that building a business took time, and you have to go through a bit of a tough time before you really start to make money, but things were going well and I was in the lucky situation that Michael's wage could support us.

As I oversaw each wedding, I continued to make detailed notes and think about how I could do things even better. I refined my website and tweaked my marketing material and services. I was feeling really positive about things and had even made my first 'public appearance' as a wedding planner – a talk at the local Women's Institute!

I'd wondered if the initial flood of enquiries would die away and I'd be left stranded, but it hadn't happened yet. Brides were starting to recommend me to their friends, and things were ticking along nicely.

It was around this time that I received an invite to attend a wedding planners' lunch. It had been arranged by a group of London wedding planners who wanted to start an association for wedding planners in the UK. I suspected that they also wanted to check out the competition.

I'd already grasped that the wedding industry was quite small, and because the suppliers all know each other, word gets around. To my utter amazement, it seemed I was already putting a few noses out of joint.

My first indication had been four months in, when I received an email from another planner: 'You're doing so well, but be careful because this industry might not really suit you.' In other words: 'Get off my patch.'

I'd assumed my business was still pretty low key, but then a videographer who had worked at a couple of weddings I'd co-ordinated also let it slip that some of the other planners had been asking about me at a wedding fair. Apparently, there had been a few barbed comments about how my service was 'cheap', and for 'brides who couldn't afford a good planner'.

So when the planner lunch invite came through, I was in two minds as to whether I should go. Yet this was an invitation to catch a glimpse of what the world of 'full wedding planning' was like. Maybe I'd even make some good contacts to boot.

The lunch took place in a function room at the Old Royal Naval College in Greenwich, and quickly confirmed my suspicions that I was a world apart from the rest of the wedding-planning pack.

Walking into the function room, it took me no time to spot what had to be the Queen Bee wedding planners. There they were, looking important and immaculate in the centre of the room, clad in their Chanel and Gucci jackets and clutching the latest Louis Vuitton totes.

As I walked over to the bar to pick up a glass of orange juice, one of the Chanel gang caught my eye. I smiled, and she looked right through me, making me feel totally small and insignificant.

Then she lowered her head and whispered to the woman next to her.

The other woman's eyes shot up, and then she started to walk towards me, quizzically eyeing my casual outfit of plain trousers and top.

This lady was impeccably dressed, in a well-tailored designer suit, accessorized with a Chanel handbag and expensive-looking high heels. After she'd looked me up and down with the accusing scowl of a customs officer, her eyes lingered on my name badge.

'Oh, you're *that* Tamryn Kirby,' she ventured in a plummy tone. 'Well, I was expecting *something* like you.'

'Oh,' I replied, raising my eyebrows. 'I don't know quite how to take that.'

'Well, you're not one of us, are you?' she clarified, indicating at my outfit. 'Do *your customers* like you dressed like *that*?' Then before I could get my reply in, she took control of the conversation. 'I don't suppose you make much,' she announced. 'Is it a little hobby for you? I cater for the *Tatler* crowd. We deal only with bespoke suppliers . . .'

After she'd reeled off a list of the most expensive and elite names and places in the business, I finally got a word in edgeways.

'But what if a bride wants something different?' I

enquired, when at last I was given time to speak. 'What if they want a different supplier?'

'Then they don't get their wedding with us,' she smiled smugly. 'Are you not getting a kickback for putting work people's way?'

'I don't do that,' I replied.

'Well, then you're missing out,' she returned sniffily, and then off she headed, back to the Gucci gaggle.

I felt utterly deflated, but quickly reminded myself that the problem was that I'd dared to make wedding planning accessible to any couple.

'Ordinary' people didn't get to have wedding planners. They were a privilege of the rich, and the industry was dominated by planners who claimed to be 'insulted' by anything less than a fifty-grand wedding.

Sadly, that wasn't the last time I met the Queen Bees.

After that, I saw them at various industry dos and wedding fairs, which I had to attend in order to meet new suppliers and, occasionally, potential clients. Through networking, I received invitations to look round venues and to the launch of new bridal ranges. And part of me wanted to keep an eye on the rivals – *and* I wanted them to see that I was still around and hadn't disappeared.

I guess there was also a part of me that just wanted to be liked and accepted. No one wants to feel like an outsider, and I thought that maybe they might start to see that the types of clients that would opt for them definitely wouldn't go for me, and vice versa. But after a while I realized I was wasting my breath. As long as I was earning a living and liked the people I worked with at my 'cheap' weddings, then what did it matter what anyone else thought?

The truth is I loved my job and I was already beginning to make some lovely friends – not least, my new buddy Julie.

Just months before, in December 2003, I'd overseen Julie's wedding, to a gorgeous guy called Julian.

When I first met them I'd liked Julie – a willowy twenty-six-year-old with a wide smile and open face – immediately. Her husband-to-be, Julian, was lovely as well, and utterly convinced he'd met me before. 'I know you,' he kept saying. 'I just can't think where from . . .'

It turned out we'd once worked for the same company, which finally put paid to Julie's constant teasing that we must have snogged in a club at some stage.

On the day of Julie's wedding, I'd left the house feeling miserable. I'd felt guilty, as Jake wasn't very well and, the day before, we'd had to have our beloved pet cat put down. I'd felt like a bad mother, but I also couldn't bear to stand Julie up. She and Julian were relying on me to make the most important day of her life go like clockwork. I couldn't let her down either.

So, reluctantly, leaving Jake with Michael, and Michael with a list of instructions, I got in my car and drove to the venue, my cheeks streaming with tears all the way.

Julie's wedding took place at Cardiff Castle and featured all the beautiful things that Julie had wanted – lovely candelabras and decorations, and all the men looking wonderful in their Welsh kilts.

Throughout the day, I was calling Michael, who informed me, to my relief, that Jake appeared to be on the mend.

Despite my worries about my son, I was glad to be there to help Julie. Although the service and reception went without drama, there was a steep staircase at the entrance and Julie needed someone to hold her dress up as she walked down it. Inevitably, during one of her many trips up and down the stairs, there was a ripping noise. Julie had put her heel through the lace trim of her dress, and a bit of material was now flapping.

Quickly bundling her off to a private room in the castle to survey the damage, I delivered my verdict.

'I think it would be best if we just cut it off,' I suggested. 'I don't think anyone will be able to tell.'

To her credit, Julie didn't seem remotely fazed, and the rest of the wedding went like a dream. There was dancing, and wonderful speeches, and gorgeous chocolate rugby balls or chocolate lollipops for the children – and the adult guests couldn't get enough of the mouthwatering chocolate-covered tower cake.

After the first dance, I was itching to get back to Jake, but when I wished Julie and Julian goodbye and drove home, a slight sadness washed over me. As brides went, Julie was divine, and I'd loved spending time with her during the build-up to the wedding. I was really going to miss her. So, a few days later, with Jake thankfully much improved, I was pleased to see I'd received an email from her.

'Hi Tamryn,' it read. 'I'm off on honeymoon today, but I'd love to take you for a drink to say thank you for everything when I get back . . .'

Two weeks later, I met her at a wine bar in Wokingham.

A few glasses of wine in, after we'd thoroughly dissected the wedding and her honeymoon, the conversation moved on to other subjects. Just normal girl stuff, but the kind of things you chat about with a friend. All of a sudden, Julie looked a bit nervous.

'Would it be weird to invite you for dinner once in a while?' she asked bashfully. 'I just feel like you've become such a part of our lives.'

'Not at all!' I laughed. 'I feel exactly the same!'

And that's how we carried on. I introduced her to Debs, who loved her from the off, and the three of us met up once a week for dinner, gossip and drinks.

Six years on, Julie is still one of my best friends, and I am godmother to her two children, who are now four and two. She knows everything about me, and it was Julie who helped me through my divorce.

What started as a business relationship has become just about as personal as you can get.

3.

Branching Out

'Happy birthday, sleepy head!' I cooed, kissing my son's cheek as he cuddled up to me, fresh from his cot and still adorably floppy.

Placing him in bed beside Michael, I ruffled his soft blond hair. Then I kissed both my boys, grabbed my bag and tiptoed downstairs, a big lump in my throat. It was Jake's second birthday, and I was spending the entire day at a wedding. I was now ten months into my wedding-planning career, and while I loved it, just occasionally those twinges of guilt would return.

For a minute I allowed my conscience to go to town. What kind of mum wasn't around for their child's birthday? I didn't need to work. I didn't have to be in this position. What was I thinking? But then I shook off the guilty thoughts. I'd painstakingly planned a party for Jake the next day. Wouldn't that make up for it?

The fact was, I loved being a mummy, but I also loved being successful at my job. I felt like a complete person again. There was no mistaking the fact that running my own business had put a spring back in my step.

Any depression I'd had after Jake's birth had now faded.

Michael was still away for work all the time, and I occupied the lonely evenings by myself with wedding organization, filling in my spreadsheets and planning ways to grow the business.

I think all the weddings I worked on gave me hope, a little glimpse into romance, and that was enough to keep me going when I felt lonely. It's about people making a new start, hoping and believing that their lives together will be something special, and that's lovely to see.

If I'm honest about it, my own marriage wasn't setting the world alight by any stretch of the imagination. Michael was away all week, and then on Saturdays I was working. I'd literally hand over Jake and rush off to a wedding. We weren't exactly lapping up the quality time together, but I figured it wouldn't be like this for ever. Wasn't this just how things were for any young couple with a child and trying to provide for the future?

I was happy enough. When you are around newlyweds-to-be all the time, you can't help but have your spirits lifted a little. Perhaps I could absorb a bit of the magic, like some kind of romantic osmosis.

While it was hard graft, there was something so thrilling about being caught up in the optimism and excitement of a marriage ceremony and the subsequent celebrations. As twee as it sounds, I've always liked problem-solving and making people happy. I loved the feel-good factor of helping people with their wedding day, and as my business expanded, it gave me the same rush that I'd experienced planning my own day. It was breathing life into me again.

I was coping with all of the unknown trials and tribulations of planning other people's weddings, many of which came down to one magic ingredient: alcohol. I soon learned to accept that dealing with retching wedding guests, or even brides or grooms, was definitely part of the job description. It's just a shame I couldn't add on a £50 additional charge for chunderers, like taxi drivers do.

No bride or groom expects to get in such a state – after all, what's the point of spending hundreds of hours and thousands of pounds planning a wedding and then not remembering anything after 'I do'? But often, a combination of nerves, not eating and then power-drinking champagne is all it takes, and the biggest peril for a newlywed is the ever-changing glass. You put it down for one second, and two minutes later it's topped up or replaced, as yet another well-wisher passes the bride a drink.

My first barfing bride came when I was just a few months into the job.

Poor Penny. Like many brides, she hadn't eaten enough dinner – probably due to a number of factors: nerves, a dress that was laced too tightly, excitement – and after necking champagne with carefree abandon, she suddenly came over all queasy.

It was her chief bridesmaid who pulled me aside to inform me that Penny was throwing up in the ladies.

I've never been great with sick; in fact, I have quite an OCD aversion to it. The sight of my toddler son vomiting was enough to have me gagging, let alone a fully grown woman. But I dutifully followed the bridesmaid into the bathroom, to see the sorry sight of Penny in all her wedding finery (complete with veil and bouquet in hand) puking like a teenager who's had too many alcopops.

Thankfully, on this occasion, the bridesmaid took control, holding her friend's hair while I passed pints of water through to them and directed guests to another loo to spare poor, puking Penny any further embarrassment.

You'll be pleased to hear that, after sitting it out for a while, Penny was able to rejoin the event. At first she looked a little wobbly, but she made a sterling recovery, to the point that her guests wouldn't have known. Indeed, by the evening, she was up on the dancefloor busting some impressive bridal moves.

Another bride who came a cropper was Carla, a petite and likable blonde in her mid-twenties.

Carla's wedding day arrived on one of those perfect summer days. There wasn't a cloud in the sky, and she looked completely radiant in her strapless taffeta gown with its hand-beaded lace bodice.

After the service, the sunshine beat down, only adding to the communal feeling of joviality as the guests mingled in the grounds of the country house where the wedding was taking place, marvelling at the mixed flower borders and woodland garden. Basking in the sun, Carla was in her element, chatting animatedly to all the guests, a permanent smile etched on her face.

But as the reception went on, I noticed that she was swaying a little. She'd previously confided to me that she had a very low tolerance to alcohol and, although I suspected that she'd had little more than three glasses, I could tell that all was not well.

As she paused to listen to what a couple in their fifties were saying, I saw that her complexion had suddenly turned a sludgy grey colour and her eyes were misty. 'Oh, God,' I thought. 'She's about to hurl.'

Time to step in. So, speed-walking across the grass, I took her by the arm. 'Come on, Carla, let's go in for a minute,' I said, pulling her in the direction of the house.

Even if I say it myself, my timing was impeccable. As soon as she was through the door and out of view of the guests, Carla clamped her hand over her mouth, made a gagging noise and ran towards the bathroom. I followed quickly, to find her on her knees in a cubicle, retching.

'It's OK,' I told her, holding her hair out of the way and moving the ruffles of her skirt to stop the vomit splashing on them. She was not in a good way.

'I don't like being sick,' she sobbed.

'I know, darling,' I soothed, rubbing her back and trying not to breathe through my nose.

Even with my hatred of puke, I felt really sorry for her. She'd clearly been having such a fun time that she'd lost track of the amount of champagne she'd drunk. That, combined with the fact that she had probably skipped breakfast and the heat of the afternoon sun, had all contributed to her sudden wave of nausea.

After dry-heaving for a while, Carla slumped against the cubicle, her eyes closed.

I handed her some water, then, when she was feeling a little better and after checking that the coast was clear, I helped her up to the bridal suite.

She immediately flopped on to the bed, her face flushed and beads of sweat on her forehead. Propping a pillow behind her, I gave her some more water, instructing her to sip it slowly. Then I ran downstairs to fetch her mother.

Carla's mum was brilliant. Grabbing a packet of cleansing wipes, she removed all remnants of running mascara; then, after instructing Carla to clean her teeth, she painstakingly reapplied her make-up.

With tears dried, new make-up applied and Carla looking decidedly more sober, we sneaked her back downstairs and, having made a pact between the three of us that no one ever need know, Carla tiptoed across the lawn to greet her groom. With our cunning story that Carla had just nipped off to have some more photos taken, no one suspected a thing.

As it happened, Carla's bout of sickness was nothing compared to what happened to another unfortunate bride I heard about who hurled all over her own wedding cake. Or the groom who was so sick over the floor of an old castle that he was put to bed at 11 p.m. Apparently, he resurfaced an hour later, bright as a button and ready to carry on drinking again, much to the disgust of his new bride and in-laws.

I even had one groom who, with the most perfect timing, managed to be sick down his shirt, minutes before he was due to take his place in church. Suited and booted in a sharp Paul Smith morning suit, he'd looked impeccable, and pretty flipping gorgeous too – that is, until the effect was ruined in one sickly second.

When he stared at me, looking all green and with an expression of pure panic on his face, I had to bite my lip. 'Oh God, what do we do now?' I groaned inwardly. 'And why, yet again, am I this close to someone else's sick!'

'Right,' I said, pointing at the usher standing closest by. '*You*, give him your shirt. Go round the corner and change. QUICKLY!'

Within minutes, they were back, the groom looking slightly better in a new shirt, and the unfortunate usher sporting his jacket, dicky bow and hairy chest as if he were a poor woman's Chippendale.

'Sorry, mate,' I sympathized. 'You'll just have to sit at the back of the church, and we'll sort you out later.'

Then I handed the groom a tissue, a bottle of water and a polo mint to freshen his breath. 'OK?' I asked.

He nodded mutely, and then the best man guided him into the church. Seconds later, the bride pulled up. Thankfully, he made it through the ceremony.

I have a theory that you can achieve a lot of calmness on your wedding day if you know what is going on – which is why, quite often, you will see grooms looking physically sick before the ceremony. The bride has done all the planning and now, suddenly, they are in the moment, with no idea of what lies in store for them. It's terrifying for them.

For a start, a lot of grooms look a little lost in their suits.

It takes a certain kind of guy to pull off a flowery waistcoat and a lilac cravat, and some look really uncomfortable. Then panic descends. The usual signs are a pale face, then beads of sweat appearing on the forehead, and then they're frantically pulling at the collar of their shirt. Before you know it, they're running around the corner of the church to retch.

If the groom hasn't had a lot of involvement in the plans and is nervous, then it's a good idea for the bride to sit down before the wedding and give him a blow-by-blow schedule of what to expect. That way, he'll have less fear of stepping into the unknown.

Of course, it isn't just the groom who can be struck with stage fright. At another wedding I did the planning for, it was just as the photographer shouted, 'Smile!' that I noticed the best man was looking a bit peaky.

Everyone had been standing up for a long time, and the photographer had just got the group into position – bride, groom, ushers and bridesmaids – for a nice shot. But just as the shutter of his camera clicked, the best man started to wobble. For a split second, he reminded me of Mr Soft from that old Trebor mint advert. It was as if all the bones had disappeared from his body and he'd turned to jelly. His knees buckled, and there he was, slumped on the grass.

As the groom and a couple of ushers crouched over him wondering what to do, I sped over. 'Let's take a raincheck, shall we?' I announced in an upbeat tone of voice, then I knelt down to tap the man's cheeks to bring him round.

With the help of a couple of guests, I managed to wake him up enough to get him to sit with his head between his knees.

Poor bloke. He'd been sweating badly all afternoon and, clearly, anxiety about his impending speech had taken its toll. He needn't have worried. When his big moment came, he pulled off a blinder.

As spring 2004 turned into summer, the season started to go into full flow and I grew rapidly busier. With the new year having brought a rush of new clients my way, I took on two more staff – Julie and Michelle.

Julie had been a co-ordinator at a prestigious Berkshire venue but left because they refused to pay her to be there on Saturdays. In what was a ridiculous situation, she'd felt so bad for abandoning her brides that she'd been turning up unpaid to her clients' wedding days. Julie was a dark-haired girl with a huge smile and a wicked laugh; she was amazing with the brides and nothing was ever too much trouble. Jackie was from London and was a slightly older lady who I could totally rely on to oversee second weddings. She was amazingly organized and never missed a trick.

As our client base grew, so did the recommendations from brides on the wedding forums, so often I'd pop up on there myself and answer questions on planning or etiquette, which would lead to more bookings.

Things were going well, but there was still room for improvement. Yet without the budget for a massive advertizing campaign and promotion, I knew I'd have to find a different way to get my message out there. That's when I had another brainwave.

Knowing that a new wedding magazine was coming out, I contacted the editor and offered to write monthly features for them. I was thrilled when she signed me up for a trial period.

After a few months, the position became permanent, and it was clear that writing these features every month gave the business an extra edge. Before long, I noticed that every time the magazine came out, there would be a flurry of hits on the website and new people would book us.

As my reputation grew, I was invited to more industry events, even giving a presentation at the prestigious Confetti store in London, which definitely raised my profile.

Before long, other magazines started asking me for quotes as well.

I also made it my task to attempt to build relationships with lots of local suppliers so they would recommend me to brides who were getting a little worried about the big day.

The business was going from strength to strength, and it was exhilarating, but also very time-consuming. I'd have my laptop on from the moment I woke up until the moment I went to bed. By now I'd enrolled Jake into nursery a few days a week, and while he was there I'd frantically try and get all my work done so that the days he was home I could make it all about him. It was easier said than done, however, and far too often I would still be tying up loose ends in the early hours of the morning.

I was living and breathing my job, so much so that often I'd be out shopping with friends when I'd be distracted by something that would be great for weddings.

Michael was relatively supportive, and he'd look after Jake on the weekends when I was at work – but I always felt he saw my job as something of a fad, something I wouldn't manage to maintain. It would never match his career in terms of importance. He was the breadwinner.

So there I was, finding my feet and getting a crash course in everything to do with weddings – including bad behaviour.

As my diary filled with wedding dates, it was becoming increasingly obvious that, on this one special day, all the usual rules of conduct were thrown out the window. And as the wedding planner, I had to deal with the fall-out.

Of all the funny, hilarious, notorious weddings I covered, one stands out in my mind as the most debauched – and it was all prompted by a specially commissioned vodka luge.

When Geraint and Imogen had first suggested having a luge, I must admit I had my reservations. Ice sculptures are a nightmare. They look great and, in theory, they are magnificent but, eventually, all you are left with is a nasty block of melting ice. Add vodka to the mixture, and it's not hard to envisage all sorts of disasters.

But, whatever my opinion, part of my business was all about knowing when to keep my gob shut. A wise wedding planner will generally smile and try their hardest to give the couple what they want. I've seen the biggest 'virtual' bitch fights you can imagine on wedding forums, all because one bride dared to label another bride's dream flower arrangement of pink carnations tacky. The fact is, one woman's trash will always be another woman's treasure. For that reason, it was my job just to nod and make things happen. You want a Smurf-themed wedding? Great! Let's do it. Bring on the blue paint!

In all seriousness, though, if I was totally convinced that something wouldn't work, I would occasionally offer up some polite reservations. 'Let me think about that and get back to you,' I'd say. Then I'd try to come up with a way of including elements of their original idea but in a way that would make it work better.

At the end of the day, you're there to put things together. I'm sure every wedding planner has seen a wedding that's just made them sigh and close their eyes, but if the client is happy, then you're doing your job.

So Geraint and Imogen got their luge, and we duly piled the Smirnoff high behind the bar.

Unfortunately, on 'luge' Saturday, the guests clearly weren't in the mood for responsible drinking – and especially not when they were confronted by a gigantic bear's head crafted from ice (no, I have no idea why you'd choose that either). In no time they had their sleeves rolled up and had loosened their ties in anticipation of sucking pure vodka off its chin.

There they remained for hours, letting off barbarian cheers as the blokes downed three shots in a row then nearly fell arse over tit slipping on the sludge gathering around their feet. Perhaps warning bells should have rung earlier, but I was first alerted to the fact that we had a real problem on our hands when a worried-looking barman scuttled over to talk to me.

'Is it all right if we stop serving alcohol to people who are too drunk?' he asked.

'What makes you think they're too drunk?' I asked back.

'Well,' he said, 'they've got through seventeen litres of vodka in the last half an hour.'

That was the cue. My eyes homed in on a man in his twenties, sitting in the corner of the marquee, swaying precariously on a chair. His tie was around his head like an SAS commando on a night out and his shirt was unbuttoned. As I watched, he leaned forward on his chair and started grappling with the carpet, picking it up and exposing the honey-coloured floorboards underneath. Never a good sign, especially as something told me he wasn't a carpenter by trade.

I could only look on in horror as he proceeded to be sick on to the bare floorboards and then drop the carpet back into place, as his table erupted in triumphant cheers. One of them thrust a drink into his hand, which he instantly started to down, his eyes rolling in his head. Ugh!

Horrified by the way things were unfolding, I immediately rallied the catering staff and asked them to put together trays with jugs of water and glasses. Then I sent them round the tables, urging the vodka drinkers to take a glass and try to sober up. It was not a pretty sight. I think

Imogen would have been really upset – if she hadn't been knocking back the vodkas herself. As it happened, she was drunkenly oblivious of her guests' appalling behaviour. As I put my plan into action, I spotted her on the dancefloor, high-kicking to 'Come On Eileen' as Geraint dribbled (possibly pure vodka) on to her shoulder.

'Well, at least they're happy,' I thought.

My next task was trying to get people home. Making the executive decision to ride the whole night out, even though I wasn't contracted to, I spent hours loading guests into cabs and plying the cabbies with extra cash in case their inebriated clients puked. Thankfully, the father of the bride had agreed to foot the bill.

I lost count of the number of times a driver commented, 'Gawd, she's plastered, isn't she?'

'Really?' I thought despairingly to myself. 'I hadn't noticed.' The rise of the free bar has a lot to answer for.

Of course, there's nothing wrong with treating your guests to a free day out – it's tradition for a lot of people, and they want everyone to relax without the pressure of paying for drinks – as long as you're aware of the potential for things to get more than a little out of hand.

There's just something about weddings that can make even the most well-behaved and polite guests go completely loopy. It never fails to amaze me how everything can change in a matter of hours.

At first, you have everyone seated in church, all sedate and smiley and looking gorgeous in their smart suits and lovely new dresses. Then, at the reception, people mingle politely, swapping stories about the couple and sharing goodwill. There are ripples of laughter, but the conversation is still a little reserved.

Fast-forward a few hours, though, and by the time you get to the first dance, it's like feeding time at the zoo.

It's normally a few drinks down the line that you start to notice the gremlins setting in. Everyone gets louder and more flamboyant, and ridiculous and outrageous behaviour becomes the order of the day. People are leering, lurching, lunging and dribbling all over the place, drinks spilling down their tops, hats being trampled on, shoes discarded; and then there's the frantic dancing, as if their lives depended on it.

Isn't it funny how nobody remembers to take pictures at the end of the night? When you get the pictures back, there are beautiful staged photos of the happy couple with their guests, rather than a group of bedraggled, beer-soaked, sweaty people all head-banging to their own personal tune, regardless of what the DJ's playing.

Still, there's nothing quite like seeing your godfather flailing his arms like he's been zapped by an electric current to 'Let's Dance' by Lady Gaga. It's all very funny.

But, sometimes, oodles of alcohol goes hand in hand with attitude. When you ask everyone to come for a group photo, there'll always be one who is too busy having a drink or a fag or just can't be bothered. Then you'll get the smart-arse who insists on rudely heckling during the speeches. While we all chortle with glee at the prospect of Bride Bianca having a bitch scrap with her estranged mother just before her latest wedding to Ricky on *EastEnders*, no one really wants to see it happen in real life, do they?

Weddings, like all big social events, can be the moment for secrets, gossip or ill feeling. Occasionally, you'll have groups of friends and people who may not have seen each other in a long time, and perhaps don't even like each other any more (or once liked each other a little too much, ahem), and here they are, getting together in close proximity and fuelled by an obscene amount of alcohol. Consequently, old disputes are picked open like scabs, bad blood comes to the boil and paranoia and resentment bubble straight to the surface.

Although it's inevitable that your average wedding has a few little 'dramas' of some sort, in my experience such minor disputes are normally low key and go unnoticed by the happy couple. Thank goodness that 'fight nights' are few and far between . . .

Maybe it was the full moon, but something strange was definitely afoot as Peter and Zoe's refined reception began to unravel at a local hotel.

Something I've always loved about weddings is that the guests adopt a kind of 'any friend of the happy couple is a friend of mine' approach. On the day, bonds are formed, jokes are swapped and merriment spreads all round. Well, that's usually the case, but on this occasion the guests appeared to have missed the memo. Instead of back-slapping and friendly smiles, many of the male guests appeared to be circling the room with their chests puffed out like peacocks and their legs stiff like bulldogs ready to sniff out a fight.

At first, I hoped they were simply single men on the lookout for a stray bridesmaid and were trying to show how manly they were in their best suits. If only.

Polite nods of acknowledgement were met by steely stares and elbowing at the bar, and as the afternoon wore on, I got the distinct feeling that something was about to kick off. Sure enough, by 8 p.m. it was like a Christmas party at the Rovers Return. Everywhere I looked there seemed to be some grief going on.

A couple arguing in the corner were getting more and more heated until, in the end, the bloke stormed off and the girl was left wailing on her friend's shoulder. Out on the veranda, another guy was being held down in his chair by peacemaking friends and force-fed fags and whiskey after threatening to 'fuck up' another guest who'd had a pop at him. Then, finally, in the mother of all rows, there was a spat between the best man and groom just after the first dance. Right in the middle of the dancefloor, where everyone had a perfect line of vision, the groom could be seen grabbing his mate by the scruff of the neck.

Suddenly, several ushers waded in, and there was lots of shouting and pushing, as the scrabble of suited and booted young men swayed precariously towards the band. The music stopped as the lead singer and bassist grabbed their instruments and headed for cover, their performance of 'Love Me Do' having been trumped by a chorus of effing and blinding. It was all rather unpleasant.

When calm had been restored and the band safely

reinstated, I discovered that the groom had 'flipped' over a disrespectful comment made in a group of the male guests, including the so-called best man, that his new wife had once been the 'village bike'. Nice.

On another occasion, which beggars belief, I witnessed a guest accusing a bride of sleeping with her husband. The woman in question was utterly convinced that her partner and the bride, who worked together, had been indulging in clandestine encounters in the stationery cupboard. But instead of doing the decent thing and saving her suspicions for a more fitting moment, she downed a glass of champagne and followed the bride into the toilets.

As several intrigued great-aunts looked on, the horrified bride of course denied all charges and promptly had her accuser ejected from the wedding. Hardly surprising really, and not the most perfectly executed interrogation, it has to be said. And whether she was guilty or not, a few minutes after the 'I dos' somehow isn't quite the right moment to bring it up – for the poor, oblivious groom's sake, if nothing else!

You'd think you'd be able to spot a pair of brawlers a mile off, but at one wedding, where two women were going at it hammer and tongs, I was surprised by how respectable they both looked.

Beforehand, they'd looked perfectly at ease, just two gorgeous girls sporting elegant dresses, carefully selected matching accessories, and handsome eye candy. But, a few drinks in, there was nothing pretty about this pair of scrubbers as they squared up to each other, snarling and hissing like a couple of territorial alley cats. Thankfully, the music was too loud to hear the full extent of their fishwife shrieking, but their body language said it all. There they were, almost nose to nose, shouting and pointing and carrying on like the chavs of the day on *The Jeremy Kyle Show*. Their alarmed boyfriends were trying their best to pull them away from one another, but with the scary strength of women scorned, they kept breaking free and heading back for more.

It turned out it was all over a work dispute. They'd previously worked together, and one had left under a cloud, which she'd blamed on the other. Yawn. This was the first time they'd met since so, naturally, they'd decided to have it out – at a wedding. Nice work, girls.

You could see the bride and groom sighing with resignation. Apparently, they'd known the risk of having them in the same room but had assumed, fairly enough, that they might button it for one night only. No such luck.

Just as the situation looked like it was going to descend into some serious scratching and hair-pulling, one boyfriend finally got a good grip of his girlfriend and managed to pull her away, bundling her outside into a taxi.

Thankfully, on that occasion, no blood was shed – which is more than can be said for the time a guest thoughtfully decided to lamp a coach driver at one of my weddings.

Now seems a fitting time to add a little word of warning for the brides out there who are thoughtful enough to lay on transportation to get their inebriated guests home: do so at your peril.

Imagine the rigmarole a kindergarten teacher endures attempting to get a class of four-year-olds, high on E numbers, on to a school bus, and then multiply it by at least a hundred. While some drunken guests are like homing pigeons, automatically stumbling out of the venue and seating themselves mutely on the bus, others are distinctly less obedient.

When one coach was arranged to ferry a group of guests to the railway station to catch the last train back to London, they hadn't counted on Great-aunt Fanny and her incessant faffing.

Every time she went to board the coach, Fanny would find another reason to stall proceedings. She thought she ought to 'spend a penny', she'd forgotten her umbrella, could she just say goodbye to her niece . . .

It's not like anyone had a train to catch or anything!

And as the time of the last train grew dangerously near, an aggrieved passenger decided he was going to take matters into his own hands. Storming down the aisle, he cleverly attempted to commandeer the bus, and when the coach driver ran up the steps to intervene, he smacked him on the nose.

The wedding had already had its fair share of problems, so when I received an angry phone call from the coach company on the Monday, I was not amused, or exactly surprised. The company was demanding a full passenger list and was threatening 'to sue'. It took all my might not to fling the phone against the wall and scream like a baby.

'I just want this wedding to go awaaaaay,' I growled, to no one in particular.

The Drunken Streets of Wedding Shame . . .

'One of my guests got so drunk that she flashed her boobs at anyone who'd look, male or female, each time she went outside to have a cigarette.'

'My sister-in-law was caught on camera doing a very sexy and knicker-revealing dance. It ended up on YouTube.'

'At my wedding, all the men, including the groom, fastened their ties around their heads and poured beer over each other.'

'A good friend, who only got married herself in April, ended up having a rendezvous in the bushes with another single friend – and I don't think they were discussing shrubbery.'

'The buffet came out at 9 p.m., and I didn't get a chance to have any of the Brie I'd chosen specially – it had literally disappeared. A straw poll of the guests revealed that no one had sampled it. I later discovered that one of my younger and drunker guests had been challenged to steal the cheese – and had managed to wedge it into his belt line and under his shirt. He danced with it there all night.'

'My teenage brother got so drunk at a family wedding that he had to be helped out of the venue by our parents. On the way, he announced he "wanted a piss" and promptly urinated all over my dad's shoes.'

'A female friend – who is not gay – kept telling me how gorgeous I looked at my wedding. Eventually, at about 3 a.m., she told me she'd quite like to shag me, and that if my marriage didn't work out I should definitely give her a call. Then she kissed me very gently on the lips and patted my bum. I thought it was a huge joke, but the following morning she sidled up and whispered, "I meant everything I said last night." Then she winked and walked away.'

Of course, it's not always the adults you have to watch.

At one wedding, I lifted a tablecloth to discover three hiccupping kids aged six, seven and ten hiding under the table necking wine. It transpired that they'd mine-swept the surrounding tables after the meal and were busy gulping from bottles of Merlot and Chardonnay.

Under-age drinking aside, weddings are always a hotbed of opportunities for embarrassment. Of course, the best man's speech often leaves the groom with a red face, but you'd be amazed by the amount of guests who are hell-bent on leaving the newlyweds blushing – particularly the groom.

With so many people in one room who know your shameful or most secret stories, there's definitely scope for some serious humiliation.

I'll never forget the poor groom who happened to be quite religious and had chosen to remain a virgin until his wedding night. Unfortunately for him, all of his friends knew about it.

Trying to head off any potential for pranks, the groom spoke to the DJ and gave him strict instructions that certain songs were categorically off the playlist, 'Like a Virgin' being top of the list.

'If anyone asks you and you play it, I will kill you,' he told the DJ with a smile. We could both tell that he wasn't joking.

It was a canny pre-emptive strike as, sure enough, through-out the night, a parade of the groom's friends approached the DJ begging him to play that very Madonna track.

Another great set-up came during the best man's speech. The best man in question was fabulously deadpan, and when he started talking about how the couple in question wanted to have an eco-friendly wedding, nothing seemed amiss.

Next came the line about wanting to reduce their carbon

footprint while on honeymoon. Again, no alarm bells. Then the best man announced to everyone that the groom was taking the bride on a romantic and exotic week away to fabulous . . . Wales!

The bride's face fell momentarily and she blurted out, 'No, no, we're supposed to be going to St Lucia.' To which the best man clapped his hand over his mouth and said, 'I'm so sorry, Jo, but when I asked Andy about your honeymoon, he just said, "I'm going to Bangor for two weeks."' The entire room (grandparents included) burst out laughing.

There are also a lot of horror stories about guests trying to sneak into the bride and groom's first-night room to 'decorate' it in a 'funny' way with things in the bed – shaving foam over the mirrors, for example, or even the odd blow-up sheep in the bath. I developed a knack of holding on to the key for the bride and groom myself, or telling the venue to give the key only to the bride or to me. It's easy to mix up any guy in the posh suit for the groom, but there's only one woman in a big white dress!

While there's always leeway for a bit of naughty behaviour, admittedly, sometimes, jokes can be taken too far.

Take the wedding where the guest of honour was a religious missionary. It was clear that the family were really proud to have him there and would happily parrot to anyone who'd listen about how he was doing great work in Africa. A bit repetitive, yes, but why not let them have their moment?

Unfortunately, what followed was a rather unpleasant drunken prank, when one male guest ran up to the missionary and grabbed his groin. 'I hear you're really big in Africa,' he quipped. It transpired that a group of lads had been attempting to embarrass the groom all day and this was their *pièce de résistance*. Ha bloody ha. I think the deafening silence echoing around after this 'hilarious' joke spoke volumes.

Over my years as a wedding planner, I've seen it all. Uncles dirty-dancing with too-sozzled-to-care young ladies while their disgusted wives look on; best men prowling the room until they find someone drunk and loose enough to salivate over; and couples playing a lot more than footsie under the table. But by far the most shocking sight was that of an impeccably well-groomed, er, lady fellating another guest right outside the marquee.

You'd think that a really high-class society wedding would see the guests conducting themselves with grace and formality, but it was actually quite the opposite.

The wedding itself was breathtaking, with a huge budget of around £150,000 spent on it. It was held at an amazing venue, the marquee looked stunning, and they even had security guards there. The guests were elegant and chic, with accents that could cut glass – but once they'd had a few, it was a whole different story.

They say the real person comes out when you drink alcohol, and if that was the case with this lot, God help them.

The dancefloor was filled largely with men who were

dancing incredibly badly to Justin Timberlake, and I was just stifling a laugh at two Sandhurst types camping it up when I saw a security guard beckoning me over.

'I need you to come outside,' he said. 'There are two people out there, and I think I need a woman to help . . .'

Puzzled, I followed him, and stepping outside it soon became very apparent what the problem was. There, right in front of our eyes, was a female guest on her knees giving her male companion a blow-job. They obviously thought they were being subtle, as they'd moved about ten feet away from the marquee, but it was pretty obvious to any passer-by what was going on. So, approaching tentatively, I coughed to alert them.

'Sorry to interrupt,' I said, trying to avert my eyes. 'But the bride and groom are about to do their last dance . . .'

If the woman was fazed, she didn't show it. Instead she remained on her knees, and slowly turned her immaculately coiffed head towards me.

'Darling, I'm terribly sorry, but I'm still hungry,' she said in a voice that would cut crystal.

She may have been cool with it, but judging by the physical reaction of the guy, it was the biggest passion-killer ever. He clearly wasn't so excited after that.

Either way, Plummy wasn't concerned. With a flick of her hair, she swanned off into the marquee, air-kissing other guests with cries of 'Darling!'

I couldn't help a quiet smirk – if only they'd known where she'd just been.

How to Beat the Drunken Antics

- Asking your hubby's friends to lay off the pranks is like a red rag to a bull. After all, you are the siren who stole him away from single life. If you are really worried that foul play may be afoot, it's worth alerting the groom's father. Get him to have a quiet word with the lads instead. They will be far more respectful.

- Try and pre-empt any potential problems before they happen and work out what you can do to defuse difficult situations. Often we don't want to think about the possibility of unpleasant things occurring, but planning for the worst-case scenario can help to prevent it happening in the first place.

- Find a way to limit the availability of the booze. If you have your wedding a bit later in the day, then you are not giving people the chance to sit around drinking.

- If you do opt for an earlier ceremony, providing a few canapés with drinks before the wedding breakfast can help absorb the alcohol.

- Make sure there are plenty of jugs of water on the tables. On a hot day, people will often neck alcohol merely because they are thirsty.

- If you are going to have alcohol on tap, think about opening the free bar after the meal. It will minimize the carnage.

I always thought one couple, Nick and Eve, had the right idea.

They were married on a sunny Saturday in Cornwall – and what could be more appropriate for pre-dinner canapés than a spot of Cornish cream tea?

Nick and Eve had planned an early wedding and were well aware of the dangers of guests drinking too much. As well as champagne and mini sandwiches, they dished out tea in lovely retro pots, with sugar cubes Nick had decorated with hearts, and served scones with cream and jam which had been sourced locally.

Everyone sat sedately on picnic rugs in the gardens of a beautiful cliff-top hotel listening to a live band, and there were no drunken antics (well, not until later anyway), just smiles all round. Consequently, the guests behaved themselves, and the wedding couple were thrilled that everyone enjoyed it so much.

Don't get me wrong: banning all booze would never

work. I still remember the year the Brit Awards banned alcohol. Seeing all those sombre, sulky celebs sitting silently without even a hint of silly, drunken revelry did not make for a good party.

That said, even though I loved my job, when you are seemingly the only sober person in the room and are being used and abused for roles such as babysitter-in-chief and general dogsbody, it can begin to grate a little.

Fuelled by Dutch courage, drunken guests would stumble over and ask me to fetch them cigarettes or even score them drugs. I know a wedding planner is supposed to do everything, but I draw the line at that!

The varying roles of a wedding planner were never-ending. If I wasn't being asked to fetch and carry for guests, they'd happily dump their children on me. Half-cut parents would instruct their kids to 'Stay with the nice lady' and head off to down sambuca at the bar.

Once, I found myself playing nursemaid to three children pretty much all day, while their parents got completely hammered. The kids were aged from three to seven, and all afternoon they followed me around. 'Can we help you?' they chirped. 'What are you doing? What's a wedding planner?'

I was used to being a bit of a kid-magnet, but I literally could not shake off these three all day. In the end I asked them to lead me to their parents. Surprise, surprise: there they were, sitting at a table under a tree that was littered with wine bottles – sozzled, as you'd expect.

'If you could keep an eye on them, that would be great,'

slurred the mother. 'We're having such a good time.' So off I traipsed, like the bloody Pied Piper.

It's not just the kids that I had to care for either. I'd often feel sorry for the elderly relatives. The whole day can be very long and tiring so I'd do my best to look after them. When everyone else was standing around necking champagne, I'd fetch them a chair and a cup of tea to stop them feeling weary. Likewise, I'd give them advance warning that it was time to head in for dinner so that they could take their time and not feel like they were holding everyone up.

I was at a lovely wedding in a stately home when I walked into one of the side rooms to find a poor old lady in a wheelchair looking very distressed. It transpired that her son and daughter-in-law had parked her up and then buggered off to enjoy the party.

'Are you OK?' I asked her.

'Not really, dear,' she replied. 'I'm terribly sorry to ask, but I'm afraid I need to use the loo, and I can't manage by myself.'

Of course, her neglectful relatives were nowhere to be found. So, wheeling her to the toilet, I used all my might to pull her out of the chair and on to the seat. I was fuming. It just seemed so humiliating for her to have to rely on a stranger to do that, all because her family were too busy enjoying the free booze and high jinx.

So, dogsbody, peacemaker, child-minder, carer – the list went on and on.

I also noticed that, quite often, guests seemed to

forget that they were not enjoying a corporate dinner, or something for which they'd paid £75 a head, or an all-inclusive holiday package. Rather, everything had been meticulously planned by their friends. When you add up all the special touches, trimmings and costs of booze and food, on average a bride and groom will pay £110 per person to have their nearest and dearest celebrate with them. Yet, unfortunately, not everyone is always grateful for the newlyweds' generosity, and this is when being the wedding planner takes on a whole new dimension – as punching bag. If the bride and groom can only afford to pay for five bottles of wine on each table, I'm the one branded stingy.

Then there is the faff of dealing with everyone's special requests and dietary requirements. Mind you, I have learned a few tricks over the years when it comes to the meal – first and foremost: always bring out the meat plates first. That way, you can avoid people suddenly going for the veggie option because it looks nicer. The last thing you want is to end up with some genuine vegetarians who still haven't had their food and all you've got left are five plates of beef.

I also set up a system where I'd put a little sticker on the place cards of genuine veggies so that the serving staff weren't hoaxed by crafty fly-by-night ones.

Some couples prefer to opt for a buffet rather than a sit-down meal, but these entail a peril all of their own. As the tables are called up to get their food in turn, invariably someone has to be last – and they're rarely happy about it.

Take one elderly relative, who decided to lead her table up in revolt, just as the caterers were changing over the joints of meat.

All you can do is keep that smile plastered on, ask people to be patient and be prepared to be whinged at.

Although most guests, in general, are completely charming, you always get a few 'difficult' ones who dance to their own tune and won't be hurried along by anyone.

Probably the most obnoxious guest I ever experienced was the woman who accused me of stealing her pashmina.

Marquee weddings are always a bit crazy, with people milling around a lot more than at formal events. It was just after the coffee and tea had been served that a tall brunette approached me.

'I hung my pashmina on the back of my chair, and now it's gone,' she slurred, her arms folded across her chest.

Funnily enough, with an entire wedding to keep on the right tracks, her pashmina was the least of my problems but, like a professional, I tried to smile and help. Big mistake.

'What colour is it – I could take a look around?' I suggested.

'Well,' she said, eyeballing me. '*You* kept walking past our table. I think you've taken it, and I want to look in *your* bag.'

Her voice was just that bit too loud, and attracted the attention of the bride, who walked over. 'What's going on?' she frowned.

'I'm sure she's got my pashmina,' the guest snapped, her

voice going up an octave. '*I want to look in her bag.*'

'Felicity!' the bride warned, aware that people were beginning to notice. 'Why on earth would Tamryn steal your pashmina?'

Rolling my eyes, I stuck out my bag. 'Here,' I said. 'Check for yourself.'

Of course, when she rummaged through, there was no sign of her blasted scarf. But, pursing her lips, she wasn't about to accept defeat. 'Well, I'm sure you've taken it,' she huffed, and walked off, leaving the bride staring at me aghast.

'I'm so sorry, Tamryn—' she started.

'Seriously, don't worry,' I smiled, even though, inwardly, I was furious. 'She'll feel silly in the morning.'

Sure enough, the following week, the bride sent me a bunch of flowers and a note apologizing for her rude guest. It turned out the wretched pashmina had been in the hateful woman's car all along.

Far from being put off by this sort of behaviour, towards the end of 2004 I decided to add a new division to the business – full wedding planning. Whereas, previously, we'd just overseen the on-the-day organization of weddings, now we were offering clients the chance to hand over the entire arrangements from start to finish if they so wished. We'd find the venue, sort out the suppliers and organize every spit and cough.

I'd worked very hard to get to this point, and had spent a lot of time researching suppliers, learning about different religions and cultures, and honing my services. After every wedding, I'd sit and write a short analysis of the event – what worked, what could work better, what I'd learned and what I could do differently next time.

I'd kept index cards on all the suppliers I'd worked with, detailing my impressions of them, information on their services and the areas they worked in so that I would have written notes on everything made while things were still clear in my mind. On top of that I'd taken a course in marketing and PR to learn how to promote my company more effectively, and I had come up with and implemented a plan of monthly press releases which I wrote and distributed.

Our on-the-day service had been such a success that it made sense to branch out. I had a good reputation, brides knew I'd been around for a while and I had lots of testimonials to reassure potential clients they were entrusting their wedding to someone who knew the territory.

Since I'd been trading, I'd noticed that more and more couples were turning to wedding planners, and while budgets were rising, people seemed to have less time to organize their nuptials.

There has also been a huge rise in the number of civil ceremonies, with couples choosing a gorgeous castle or stately home rather than getting married in their local area. This meant that having someone 'on the ground' near their wedding venue who knew local suppliers and could attend meetings on their behalf was a huge plus, especially for people busy with work.

So I took the decision to rebrand the business, and called it TK Weddings. Then I sent out a press release to all our clients and all the suppliers, letting them know that the company was now offering more than just 'on-the-day' co-ordination; full planning and design were available as well.

Despite the extra work the rebrand and branching out involved, I loved it. It was a new challenge, and I wanted to push myself to see just how much I could achieve. I found an immense sense of satisfaction in earning money from my own business, which was completely unlike anything I'd had when I was receiving a regular paycheck. I'd done all this myself, and it was a great feeling.

Although Michael didn't object to the expansion, I don't think he was as convinced as I was that I would make it work. During the snatched conversations we had on the rare days or nights he was home and I wasn't working, he'd listen and then just nod.

But I had faith that I would make it work. I had prepared, researched and learned lots of new skills to help me build on the good reputation I had already gained.

Ironically, after some of my rival planners had turned their noses up at my on-the-day service, a fair few had gone on to copy it – one even reproducing my description of the service almost word for word on her website! When I sent her a 'friendly' legal letter asking her to remove it, of course it was all blamed on her web designer.

Now my decision to branch out into full planning was clearly being watched, and I could tell from my web stats that lots of planners were keeping a regular eye on my website.

Wedding planning might come across as a fluffy, happy, lovely business, but there is definitely a cut-throat element to it. It's not unknown in the industry for a planner to use a friend to book a 'fake' consultation with a marriage planner in order to get a full proposal and sample contract to find out what competitors are up to, and I think that happened to me at least once.

But whether there were spies lurking or not, I was confident that we had the right approach to make a success of the full planning. While some wedding planners would happily charge 10 or 15 per cent of whatever the final wedding budget would be for their full planning services, I decided to base our fee on the amount of work we would be doing. I'd go to a meeting with the bride and groom and talk through all the details: where they wanted to get married, what things they wanted to include, etc. Then, once I'd heard their requirements, I'd suggest services that would be of use to them. Based on how much would be involved, the fee could be anything from £2,500 to more than £15,000.

Once again, there was lots of learning on the job, and I soon realized it was important to spell out that I wouldn't be attending every single meeting with suppliers and every dress fitting. Likewise, if a couple wanted me to sort out RSVPs, then there would be an extra charge. I had to make it clear from the outset, or people would just assume I was willing to do these things, but I definitely learned that the hard way.

One of the first full weddings I did was for a couple who had asked me to arrange accommodation for guests flying in from overseas. I'd included this in my costings but then, as the time grew closer, it was clear they expected me also to arrange guest transportation from the airports to the hotel and for welcome baskets to be put in each of their rooms.

Similarly, I got caught out with a bride and groom who expected me not only to come with them to a series of cake-tasting sessions but also to collect them from the station and drive them between meetings.

On both occasions I hadn't been clear enough about what I would and wouldn't do, so I had backed myself into a corner.

After these two experiences, I completely overhauled the way I wrote our proposals, and I made sure all the small print was there accordingly.

With TK Weddings now responsible for overseeing the full shebang at weddings, another of my chief concerns was making sure that the venues I'd developed a good working relationship with were treated with respect by the guests.

A surprisingly frequent problem was reining in the light-fingered antics of the more sozzled guests. In my student days, I recall daft friends stealing anything for a laugh after a few too many Bacardi Breezers: traffic cones, beer mats, pint glasses – you name it. But if I thought drunken kleptomania was something people grew out of, I soon got a wake-up call when I started wedding planning.

You wouldn't believe the things I've caught paralytic

wedding guests trying to steal. I once caught a woman trying to shove a cushion into her coat.

'But they won't need it once the wedding is over,' she insisted, as if I was the one being unreasonable.

'Yes, but it actually belongs to the venue,' I replied, trying my hardest not to grit my teeth. 'So let's put it back now and forget this ever happened, okay?'

Basically, after five glasses of champagne and however much wine, the rule is: if it isn't nailed down, then it might be pinched.

I've spied guests scooping up decorations, candles, even chair covers; and if the specially crafted wedding favours are left behind by forgetful guests, you can guarantee some greedy sod will go round the room scooping them into their handbag.

Fancy handwash and hand cream go missing from the toilets, vases from the tables – with and without the flowers in them – and you can be virtually certain that someone at least among the guests will wander off with a bottle of wine.

The most comical thief I ever encountered was the groom's granny, who was seen walking rather oddly when she was leaving the marquee. When one of the ushers ran to her aid, she was very cagey and tried to turn down his offer of help. There was a bit of a flap as she attempted to rebuff his chivalry but then, as he took her arm, she dropped her coat.

It crashed to the ground with a big smash as the champagne bottle she'd tried to sneak out shattered all over the wooden floor. Surveying the damage, she hobbled on regardless, another bottle clearly stashed up her top. As I stood watching with the bride and groom, the three of us just cried with laughter.

It's stories like this that will never lose their comedic value, and they pretty much sum up why I will always love weddings.

4.

Simply the Best

'Tamryn, you're a wedding planner – what do you think?' Robert Kilroy-Silk demanded, bounding towards me.

Suddenly I was aware of the mike boom looming in above my head and bright camera lights hot on my face. Yikes!

When I received a call from the *Kilroy* television programme asking me if I'd come on to talk about whether people spend too much on weddings, I'd immediately said yes, then panicked for two reasons. Firstly, how on earth would I get my son to nursery, as yet again Michael was away on business? And, secondly, what on earth would I wear?

The following morning, with a friend drafted in for nursery duty and a bout of emergency late-night outfit shopping under my belt, I sat terrified in the back of the car they'd sent to pick me up, frantically preparing 'interesting' and 'spontaneous' things to say.

When I arrived, I was quickly wired up with a mike and placed on a rather uncomfortable sofa between a wedding DJ and a vicar.

As it turned out, most of my preparation was completely in vain. When my big moment arrived, it lasted all of about five seconds. When Kilroy fired the question at me, I cleared my throat.

'Um, well, some people do let things get out of perspective and spend a lot of money on their weddings . . .' I began.

The vicar next to me nodded furiously in agreement. But Kilroy was already off again, running up the stairs to a more interesting and outspoken guest.

Oh well, at least I made a good impression on the vicar.

After that, my TV appearances happened more regularly. My magazine column led to appearances on *GMTV* and *Lorraine Kelly Today*, and I even went on *BBC Breakfast* to talk about Prince Charles and Camilla's wedding.

I always found it a bit of a bizarre experience. They'd kind of wheel you on, you'd say your bit and then they'd wheel you out again. It was a feat of organization that certainly impressed me, as I'd get only a few minutes to gulp a coffee before someone was tucking wires down my top. If I did a segment on breakfast TV, I'd go to the studio, have my hair and make-up done, deliver my soundbite and be out and back home with a full face of make-up on by 9 a.m. It was all so slick.

And there was no doubt it made a big difference to the business. After every excursion to the TV studio, I'd come home and check my website statistics to see how many people had logged on after my minute on screen. The numbers would be huge, not just a few extra hundred, but thousands more and, as a result, the commissions kept rolling in. To cope with the workload, I took on another four members of staff.

First, there was George, a bride whose wedding I'd co-ordinated, who was based in Gloucestershire. She was blonde, smiley and brilliant, and as ex-Virgin cabincrew, she could handle anything. Next, I hired Anna, who lived in Bedfordshire, a gorgeous girl with dark ringlets and a big laugh who was impeccably organized.

Phoebe, a tall, willowy blonde, was my one recruitment mistake. I took her on as she was based down near Bristol, which was an area we were getting lots of enquiries for, but eventually we parted company. As you can imagine, I was less than impressed to discover that, after I'd trained her up, she'd immediately started her own wedding-planning school!

Lastly, there was Tess, another bride whose wedding we'd co-ordinated. She was a wonderful, happy girl based in Surrey who, thankfully, never let me down.

Although I didn't pay a regular salary to the girls and they received a fee per job, I did feel quite a lot of pressure to keep bringing in new contracts for them all. Some of them were already working full time in the week and did the weddings to help with financial problems; others did it because they were bored with their 'day' jobs; and some just wanted to be wedding planners but openly admitted they didn't want to run their own business.

I spent a lot of time training them up and then dealing with their queries about how to handle or answer enquiries from the bride. Expanding the company created a huge amount of work for me, and I was working late into the night most evenings, but I was determined to make a go of it and to prove that I could run a successful business, to myself as much as to anyone else.

One of the many suggestions I imparted to my staff was never to oversee a wedding with a hangover. To be honest, the tasks that presented themselves were often taxing enough with a clear head.

Have you ever tried wrestling a tight, stretchy cover over a chair? You experience the same frustration you feel when you're struggling to manoeuvre a fitted sheet into place without it springing back off the corners of the mattress and ending in a messy tangle in the middle of the bed. Now imagine having to repeat the same feat for 150 beds – and with a stonking great hangover. Ugh.

When a bride asks sweetly, 'Could you just pop the chair covers on for me? Oh, and don't forget the matching bows as well,' you definitely need to be firing on all cylinders.

And who needs a hangover when you know you've got to spend sixteen hours on your feet with no guaranteed break? And how about dealing with the pounding disco while your own head is banging along in time as well? Much too painful, I can tell you.

I once wore a pedometer during a wedding to measure how far I walked during the day, and by the time I flopped back into my car late that evening, it was almost at twelve miles. Sod the gym membership!

Wedding planning was certainly putting me through my paces, but the buzz I got from a job well done made it all worthwhile. I loved the challenge of dealing with whatever the wedding gods chucked at me. I was constantly having to think on my feet, especially if there was a potential inferno on my hands – as was the case at one wedding I particularly remember.

During the wedding breakfast, we'd decorated the tables with tea lights to create a nice, soft effect. It looked lovely, but then the bride's mother pulled her menu from her napkin and held it over the candle to read it. Squinting at it, she was completely oblivious to the fact that the naked flame from the candle was in dangerous proximity to the cardboard menu.

In a matter of seconds, she'd not only set the menu on fire but had also dropped the burning card on to the tablecloth, which also went up in flames. For a split second I was lost in memories of that episode of *Sex and the City* where Miranda makes a toast at Charlotte's wedding and her bit of paper goes up in flames, then I realized it was time to jump into action.

As the bride's mother recoiled in horror, I dashed forward to grab a glass of water, which I used to douse the flames. It left an unsightly hole in the tablecloth, but at least the guests weren't being evacuated from a burning marquee!

Then there was the grandmother who forgot the heirloom knife which the bride and groom were meant to cut the cake with. It might have been fine if only she'd owned up earlier on.

The wedding ceremony was taking place at a beautiful

church in Oxfordshire; then the guests were making their way back to a stunning marquee reception in the grounds of a country house.

That afternoon, I'd gone to the ceremony, while Julie, with whom I'd teamed up for the day, had stayed at the venue to co-ordinate the caterers and the arrival of the entertainment. As the guests filed out of the church after a flawless ceremony, I was just contemplating how well everything was going when I was approached by a beaming lady in her eighties.

'I'm the grandmother of the bride!' she told me proudly.

'I'm so pleased to meet you,' I replied, remembering that this must be the granny who was bringing a special knife which she'd used to cut the cake at her own wedding, as had the bride's mother. 'I can't wait to see the cake knife.'

'Ah,' she said, grabbing my hand to whisper in my ear. 'The thing is, dear, my memory is not what it was and I'm afraid it slipped my mind to bring it.'

Immediately I had one of those moments when your insides just go cold, and under my suit I got incredibly hot, but I smiled, patted her hand and told her it wasn't a huge problem. 'We'll sort it out,' I assured her.

So, disappearing around the corner with my mobile phone, I called Julie and asked her to see if the caterers had brought a cake knife.

'No, they haven't,' she told me after she'd been to investigate. 'They'd been assured by the bride that there was no need, as she'd be using her own.'

Oh Lord.

Back at the venue, Julie and I grabbed the Yellow Pages and frantically started calling round every cake shop we could find. It was now approaching 3 p.m., and a lot of them had closed for the day. It took a long time but, finally, Julie found one that was still open and had a cake knife that we could buy.

Jumping in her car, she drove like a madwoman to the shop, bought the knife and raced back to the venue so as to be there when the bride and groom arrived.

They were completely gracious about the whole thing. Indeed, when the grandmother apologized, the bride just laughed it off and said, 'Well, perhaps we'll start a new tradition with this knife.'

In a nice touch, they've since used it to cut the christening cake for their first baby.

Meanwhile, Julie and I both added cake knives to our 'emergency kit' for weddings after that.

The Wedding Planner's Emergency Kit

1. Baby wipes – sounds absolutely mad, but a swipe over a stain with one of these will usually make things better. Perfect for messy flower girls. Also, a stick of white chalk can cover little marks on the bride's gown.

2. A clothes peg – to 'peg' the veil to the back of the bride's dress if it's windy and so avoid photos of the bride being strangled by her own veil. Also, if it's been wet, a sheet for the bride to stand on during the photos will avoid getting the bottom of her gown muddy.

3. Rescue® Remedy – the best emergency pick-me-up for brides, grooms, best men and guests feeling the strains of the day.

4. Insect repellent – sweet drinks and sticky canapés are a magnet for mozzies in the summer months. Don't end your big day covered in bites.

5. Suntan cream – standing around in a strapless dress for photos and drinks can lead to sore, red shoulders, and that's to be avoided at all costs.

6. Mini safety pins – a quicker, less fiddly way to fix little rips and tears than trying to sew. Great for hems on trousers and sashes on dresses.

7. Pens, double-sided sticky tape, Blu-Tack and scissors – always useful for last-minute jobs, wrapping gifts, writing cards, securing decorations, trimming ribbon . . .

8. Comb, hair grips and hairspray — essential for quick fixes to hairdos. Similarly, face powder and lipstick for pre-photo pampering.

9. Blister plasters — because new shoes and a day of standing up can give even the most glam of brides distinctly un-glam blisters.

10. Spares — of anything that you're using. Spare tea lights, batteries (for fairylights, guests' cameras, etc.), and definitely spare hold-up stockings in case of pulls. Also, spare copies of the directions from the church to the reception are helpful for guests without sat-nav.

With a first-aid qualification under my belt, I was also constantly primed to leap into action should a best man faint or a guest accidentally maim themselves on a broken champagne glass. Then there were the frail, overcome grannies; the hobbling and wincing guests who'd been trampled on by a rogue stiletto on the dancefloor; and the terminally accident-prone.

Although I thank my lucky stars that I never encountered a life-threatening medical emergency at any of the ceremonies I covered, there was one worrying episode in Scotland where we had to call in the air ambulance.

On that memorable day, the wedding ceremony was taking place in a room in a castle tower, which could only be reached by a steep, spiralling staircase. It was quite a work-out for anyone who made it up the steps and, obviously, there was no lift.

It was stifling during the service, and soon the small room, which was full of hot, perspiring bodies, got really, really musty and humid. The service just seemed to go on for ever, and everyone was shifting uncomfortably in their seats, mopping their brows and removing layers of clothing in a fruitless attempt to cool down.

I'd already opened the windows in the hope of a cooling breeze, but it had little effect. The gaggle of well-turned-out guests was becoming distinctly damp around the edges.

It was just before the end of the service that I saw a man in his forties had slumped in his seat, out for the count. His wife was crouched down next to him, lightly slapping his cheek and attempting to rouse him.

I walked over quietly and joined her in trying to wake him up. But as I stood there, frantically fanning him with the order of service, he remained unconscious. Thankfully, he was at the back of the room, so the bride and groom were able to carry on with their vows, unaware of the drama in the corner.

When he eventually came round, he barely focused on us before his eyes rolled back in his head and he passed out again. When the service came to an end and everyone filed out of the room, he was still in much the same state, with no sign that he was about to get any better. So, after a further ten minutes, I called for an ambulance.

Because of the remote location, they sent an air ambulance, and we didn't have to wait long before you could hear the propeller blades of the helicopter echoing around the castle.

A short while later, two men in green paramedics uniforms came trudging up the stairs armed with bags of medical paraphernalia and cylinders of oxygen, and started to treat him.

Our sickly charge had recovered slightly with the oxygen but was still very floppy, and we were now faced with the task of getting him down that steep spiral staircase. As the poor ambulancemen heaved him down a seemingly never-ending staircase I tottered behind carrying the oxygen cylinders. By the time we reached the final step, we were all sweating like no one's business.

The man was taken to hospital and mercifully made a full recovery.

As well as the perils of sudden illness, another thing you have absolutely no control over is what Mother Nature may have in store.

The drawback of a summer wedding is that you can become hell-bent on the weather being perfect and having your drinks outside, only to have it all descend into a soggy mess with one ominous clap of thunder. Even if you're all set for a roasting August day, it's important to look at the compromises available should the heavens open.

Gardens are lovely, but if you can't use them, will you be stuck in a formal function room or will your venue have somewhere with a bit more personality to move the party to? If you have a contingency plan, then there's no reason why your wedding can't be every bit as wonderful as you wanted – weather permitting or not.

One rain-plagued bride managed to smile through the torrential downpour on her wedding day because, despite having to shelve her plans to use the gardens of a stately home, her guests were treated to an impressive afternoon tea in the main house.

'It might have poured all day, but the house was gorgeous and everyone was completely awestruck,' she said afterwards. 'Plus, the light was really beautiful for the photos.'

I can remember another wedding in a marquee where it seemed like the rain gods were unleashing all hell on us.

The wedding was taking place at the bride's parents' farm, and the field that housed the marquee was rapidly getting very muddy and boggy. Everything was soaking wet, and sinking into the ground. To make matters worse, it rained so hard before the celebrations that the tent was leaking, and we spent the entire morning attempting to mop up the dancefloor.

The caterer's van's wheels were slipping and sliding as they tried to make their way across the field to set up the barbecue the bride had booked while dreaming of soaring temperatures and cloudless skies.

Thankfully, thinking ahead the day before, the bride and groom and their family had rung round all the guests they could instructing them to bring wellies. So after the church service, we were met with the funny sight of guests in sharp suits and gorgeous dresses stepping out of their cars in wellies and staggering across the mud clutching their best shoes and stilettos. Then, by the door of the marquee, a massive stack of boots began to pile up as people swapped over their footwear.

Sadly, the rain failed to let up all day, so the photographer quickly whipped everyone outside for a speedy group photo – everyone smiling despite the wind and rain.

As people got drunker, it soon became a hilarious free-for-all as people grabbed the first odd boots they could lay their hands on and lurched outside to find the loos. I think love might even have blossomed between a chivalrous usher and a slightly soggy guest when he used his coat to shelter her as she ran to her car to collect the card and gift she'd bought for the happy (if slightly damp!) couple.

The final palaver happened when the guests attempted to leave. Car after car got stuck, wheels spinning in the mud, until the bride's brother saved the day by towing them out of trouble with his tractor – Farmer Giles to the rescue!

By the end, the marquee was decimated, with the expensive cream carpet that had been laid down specially completely trashed. Likewise, the poor bride's dress was grey at the bottom and her dainty silk shoes wrecked.

It might not have been the wedding she'd dreamed of, but there was no doubt that having to battle the elements had left everyone fired up and given them a real sense of camaraderie. It was certainly a wedding that everyone enjoyed and would talk about for years to come.

For every couple who find themselves fighting against the weather, though, there will be another lucky enough to have a glorious summer's day.

After all the fun at the farm I was blessed with the August 2005 wedding of Nicola and James. As couples go, these two were completely loved up, and to this day they will remain two of the nicest clients I have ever worked with.

As luck would have it, they'd picked a fabulous summer's day to tie the knot, at Nicola's childhood church.

It was one of those memorable weddings as, not only was the setting beautiful, but Nicola had excelled herself with gorgeous touches throughout – not least a lovely horse-drawn carriage to take them through the stunning scenery of the New Forest to their reception in Beaulieu.

But the day before the wedding, we were suddenly faced with a dilemma. The roads James and Nicola would be travelling along into the New Forest had cattle grids. How on earth were we going to get the horses through?

So, in a farcical situation, on the morning of the wedding Julie and I could be found getting all kinds of weird looks from passers-by as we laid huge pieces of cardboard over all the cattle grids along the route.

'I bloody hope this works,' I remember saying to Julie with a grimace as we laid the slabs of corrugated cardboard across the metal bars.

Later, back at the venue, I waited nervously for the bride and groom.

At last, I heard the distant sound of clip-clopping grow

nearer and nearer until finally the horses rounded the corner and I spied an ecstatic-looking Nicola beaming from the carriage. Hurrah!

All in all, it was a wonderful wedding. Nicola had arranged activity packs to keep the children amused and had picked little heart-shaped stones as favours. There were petals sprinkled up the stone steps to the dinner and dancing, along with pretty candles flickering and giving off a romantic glow. It just looked divine.

And in an additional special touch, the newlyweds had asked all their guests to become popstars for the day on their wedding video.

After the dinner, the bridesmaids circulated with copies of the lyrics for Lou Reed's 'Perfect Day' and a portable CD player, and encouraged pairs of guests to mime a few lines each for the videographers. All the clips were then pieced together to create a complete video of the song. It took a lot of work, but it looked amazing in the end.

The newlyweds had also not forgotten a single person in their speeches, and everyone who had contributed to the day was thanked and called up to receive a little gift. It was my job to work my way through the massive stack of gifts on a table to the side of the bride and groom and make sure that they had exactly the right package to hand at exactly the right moment. It was quite a task, and no one was left out.

The following day, again in a lovely touch, Nicola, who was determined to make the most of her time with her nearest and dearest, even organized a big picnic in the New Forest for all her guests. The direction cards everyone was given to guide them to the picnic site featured photos of Nicola and James at various landmarks along the way and, once they'd arrived, the guests had fun with food, drink and games. It doesn't get much better than that!

Unfortunately, the next summer wedding I oversaw was gatecrashed by some unwanted and unexpected guests. If you're planning to have your wedding at that time of year, don't forget to make contingency plans for the possible invasion of creepy-crawlies.

The wedding took place on one of those heavy and humid August days in need of a good thunderstorm to clear the air. Sadly, right on cue, just as the reception drinks were being served, a black cloud moved in threateningly towards the guests.

Suddenly the sky was filled with a haze of bugs, and people were frantically flapping their hands in front of their faces and running into the marquee to escape the swarm. It was like a plague of locusts, with insects crawling over everyone.

Scrabbling in my emergency kit, I immediately began to hand out all the insect-repellent wipes I could find and deposited citronella candles all around to try and ward off the tiny pests. It was all pretty fruitless, to be honest!

Women in strappy dresses were shrieking as midges crawled on their arms and shoulders and got stuck to their gloss-smeared lips; everyone had itchy ankles and the bride was bitten all over her back. At one point we had to take her veil off, as so many of the little pests were getting caught up in it.

The barbecue grill for the food kept them at bay for a bit, but the ankle-nibbling was pretty much unrelenting for the entire wedding. When I got home that night, I discovered that I too had been bug food and had big bites on my legs.

I didn't think much could top that unpleasant brush with nature – that is, until I oversaw a wedding at Hampton Court House, which has the most gorgeous rustic gardens.

The bride in question wanted to make the most of the garden area during the evening, especially as it was quite warm. So, during the dinner, I'd gone outside to hang lanterns in the trees, put hurricane lamps with candles along the pathways and set tea lights on the tables outside.

I was standing in a flowerbed tucking tea lights into the alcoves of a wall when, out of the corner of my eye, I caught sight of something moving. Looking down, I saw a massive grass snake slithering through the flowerbed, about a metre away from me. Pretty scary for the average person, but absolutely bloody terrifying for a confirmed snake phobic such as myself.

I'd never really come into contact with a snake before, but my mum had done a spectacularly good job of passing her own fear on to me. Now, with a real-life wild snake winding its way past me, I was momentarily frozen to the spot. My heart was pounding in my chest, and I heard a strange, strangled, squeaking noise coming from my mouth.

When the snake slithered off again, I picked my way out of the flowerbed and back on to the main path and sprinted (for the first time in my career, my 'no running' rule went out the window) back to the house.

Plonking myself down in the kitchen and panting like a lunatic, I begged the caterers to make me a strong cup of tea.

Unfortunately, when the bride left the dinner to go to the toilet, she saw me sitting clutching my cuppa, a shaking, jibbering wreck.

'Are you OK, Tam?' she asked. 'You look like you've seen a ghost.'

'No, not a ghost, just a snake!' I managed to squeal.

You'd think that having been an air cadet when I was younger would make me quite intrepid generally, but as well as snakes and people being sick, I had another phobia – boats. So you can only imagine my dismay when a bride requested me to oversee her pleasure-cruise reception on the Solent.

Initially, when I'd gone to talk through the wedding with Sally and Mike, a couple from Southampton, a month before the wedding, it had all sounded wonderful. As they reeled off their plans for a ceremony at Southampton Civic Centre followed by drinks, canapés and entertainment for the guests in the form of fire jugglers and other circus acts, I nodded enthusiastically.

'Then, after that, we're going to get everyone down to the docks to board *Ocean Scene*,' Sally added excitedly.

'Oh God,' I thought. 'They want me to go on the boat with them.' My stomach lurched just thinking about it.

The plan was that the boat would do a loop around Southampton Water while everyone was having drinks and dinner. Then it would return to Southampton to pick up more guests and drop a few off before heading out again for a disco at sea.

'It sounds horrendous,' I thought secretly in my head.

'It sounds brilliant,' I said out loud.

Oh Lord. How on earth was I going to survive this one?

The night before the wedding, I didn't sleep at all. I just lay there working myself into a fearful frenzy. 'Will I even be able to get on the boat?' I wondered. 'How on earth will I manage to do my job if I'm absolutely terrified?'

The following afternoon, in front of the boat, I steeled myself. Swallowing hard, I gripped the rail on the gang-plank and concentrated on putting one foot in front of the other to make my way onboard. When, twenty minutes later, the engines fired up and the boat began to move out of the harbour, I concentrated on breathing deeply to control my panic.

It wasn't actually as bad as I'd thought it would be, and having a task at hand helped to stop me freaking out – although I did get through quite a lot of Rescue® Remedy that day. Thank goodness for my emergency kit!

I also realized that my slightly shaky walk could easily be craftily attributed to the movement of the boat. Devious.

Even though I wasn't sick, a couple of guests were adding to my discomfort. If a snake had popped up, it would have been a hat trick!

After having checked my watch every ten minutes, I was thrilled when the boat finally moored up back at the harbour and Sally finally gave me the green light to leave. I practically sprinted off that boat, vowing to myself that never in a million years would I agree to a boat-based reception to any of my clients.

In recent years, the unpredictability of the British summer weather has led to a real surge in winter ceremonies, and I've always liked them. With no expectations of warmth or sunshine, the whole occasion is usually a much more relaxed affair, and even when it's unbearably cold, you can add heat and make everything snug and cosy.

In December 2005 I oversaw one of my favourite winter weddings, belonging to a wonderful couple called Mark and Jess, who'd really gone to town with their festive theme. The tables at their dinner were decorated with rich reds and golds and had all been given a Yuletide name, for example, mistletoe, holly and ivy. A huge Christmas tree in the banqueting hall made a fantastic centrepiece, and the candles and fairylights around the room created a magical atmosphere.

Best of all, during the speeches, there was an 'interruption', with the ringing of a bell and a massive 'Ho ho ho' coming from outside the banqueting hall. Santa Claus then burst through the door, to massive whoops of excitement, and proceeded to hand out presents. I suspect some of the adults were more excited than the children.

The only trial of the day came as everyone began to leave and had to battle their way through the thick fog that had descended on the venue. That night, I was gripping the steering wheel of my car with nerves as I drove slowly through the dense fog of the New Forest. It was really eerie.

Although I got home unscathed, the videographer wasn't so lucky – she called me the next day to say she'd crashed her car into a ditch!

As 2005 came to an end, I gained four more members of my team.

There was Jenny in Shropshire, a bouncy little blonde thing with the most amazing green eyes; Kate in Buckinghamshire, the sort of girl you could call for help in the middle of the night; Karen in Dorset, who was gorgeous with the most fabulous dark-brown corkscrew Julia Roberts curls; and Lucy, based in Devon, who was only twenty but wise beyond her years.

By now, business was split 50/50 in terms of full planning and our on-the-day service. Although the value of the full-planning weddings seemed to increase almost with each booking, I didn't want to turn my back on the on-the-day stuff. Our initial service was what had made us different and kept us in touch with 'real' brides, and it was a wonderful way to meet new suppliers and venues.

The next year started brilliantly when I was named Best Wedding Planner at the Wedding Awards.

When I heard we'd been shortlisted, I wanted to really impress the judging panel of industry professionals, so I'd spent hours putting together massive display boards and filled them with lots of pictures and testimonials from all our clients.

The Wedding Awards were a huge deal, with a massive media announcement, and emails immediately started to flood in with congratulations from suppliers and venues we'd worked with, as well as from clients, past and present. I was called up by local radio and TV stations, and was also asked to do photocalls for the local newspapers, clutching my winner's prize.

But although my business associates, clients, friends and my mum made a massive fuss of me, one person's enthusiasm was noticeably missing. My husband, the guy I'd name-checked as 'my biggest supporter' in my own wedding-day speech, didn't even buy me a bunch of flowers or a card to say congratulations. It really hurt my feelings. Indeed, whenever I came home raving about the good things that were happening to me, he'd go a bit mute. There was no happiness, no excitement.

In the aftermath of the award, we were hit with a wave of new and interesting clients.

One of my first 'full-plan' weddings that spring was a wedding where the groom was quite the bargain-hunter. Indeed, as the weeks before the wedding flew by, I realized that there was no bigger buzz for him than the feeling that he was getting a bargain. So, naturally, when he'd stumbled across a shop that was offering a good deal on wedding jewellery, he'd immediately snapped up two wedding bands – despite only being able to estimate his fiancée's ring size. Then, for some reason, he waited until the day before the wedding for her to try it on. Lo and behold, it was too small, and at 4 p.m. on a Friday there was little hope of getting it re-sized in time.

The bride, to be fair to her, took it in her stride, and a plan was hatched. Before the best man handed over the ring in church, he'd quickly grease it up with olive oil to ease the process.

When it came to exchanging the rings on the day, the best man managed to subtly pull this off. There was a bit of a grapple as the groom attempted to slip the ring on – unfortunately, caught by the videographer, who was zooming in – but everyone just had a giggle about it, and the service continued without drama.

Well, of course, the best man was the hero of the hour – that is, until he got up to make his speech.

'Well, I never thought I'd see Graham grease Jane's ring in church,' he began.

It was a very religious wedding, and what had been, up until that point, a funny little story suddenly turned into something else. It could have been ignored, but of course there were a few stifled snorts from the younger crowd, which drew attention to the poor-taste joke, and Graham and Jane turned scarlet.

Not long after this, I was looking after the wedding of a bride who had her heart set on a platinum wedding ring, and she was in luck: the groom duly went out and bought one, making a big thing of having fulfilled his wife-to-be's wishes.

The wedding ceremony passed without drama, but afterwards I noticed that she kept fiddling with her finger.

'Are you having trouble with your ring?' I asked.

'I don't know if I've got my finger wet, but it's really itchy,' she explained. 'You don't have any cream, do you?'

When I took her off to examine her hand, her finger was looking a bit green and she had a rash, so we put some Sudocrem on it. Her bridesmaid poked her head round the door to see where her friend had got to. The bride held out her hand.

'Look what's happened,' she laughed. 'I hope it's not a bad omen!'

'Oh, that's what happened to my friend when she wore silver,' the bridesmaid exclaimed.

'But this is platinum!' the bride replied.

'Uh-oh,' I thought.

'Are you sure it's platinum?' the bridesmaid continued, clearly oblivious of the drama she might be creating – at which point, with perfect comic timing, the groom wandered in to find his wife, just catching the end of the conversation.

'Look, I've got a rash,' she said, showing him. Well, his face just went white.

'It's silver,' he admitted in a small voice.

The poor bride – her face fell, her shoulders dropped

and she plonked herself down on a seat looking ever so sad. Not cross, just very hurt.

'I can't believe you lied to me,' she said, her eyes filling with tears.

The groom couldn't have looked more upset either, and as he knelt down in front of her, taking her hands and whispering apologies, the big-mouthed bridesmaid and I quickly reversed out of the room to give them some time to sort things out.

I felt really sorry for the poor groom. All he'd wanted was for everything to be perfect for her. He was just mortified.

Thank goodness she forgave him, and the next week they headed to the jewellers to swap it.

While some grooms are penny-pinching others have more money than sense to throw at their nuptials, and as time wore on, we began to pick up clients with huge budgets.

When I met my first £100,000 clients, my eyes nearly popped out of my head when they casually mentioned their limit.

The consultation had felt like any other to start with. I met Matilda and Richard, who were in their mid-thirties, at their plush home in Windsor, and we sat for ages talking about the ideas they had for their wedding. They wanted something elegant, with a few fun aspects thrown in, but nothing tacky – everything should be of good quality, and they especially wanted excellent photography and entertainment.

I usually left 'the budget' question until quite late in the consultation, because I didn't want people to think that it was my main concern when that absolutely wasn't the case. So I'd been talking to Matilda and Richard for at least an hour before the subject of money was broached.

'Well,' Matilda said, looking a little flustered, 'my parents want to pay for it all, and are suggesting about £100,000. But that seems mad to us,' she added, looking embarrassed.

Once I'd got over the initial shock, I was secretly thrilled. Having the freedom of such a huge budget was very exciting for TK Weddings as it meant we could be creative in so many ways. Back home, I immediately put together a proposal and sent it to the couple for their approval.

They replied the next morning saying they'd love to work with me, and suddenly there I was looking into all the bespoke wedding suppliers. It would have been easy to get carried away, but I was also determined to get the wedding in under budget, as I didn't want to look as if I was out to spend every penny.

As a rule, I always worked with a 10 per cent contingency, which meant that, whatever the total budget, I worked everything out to spend 10 per cent less. This gave me room if the couple suddenly wanted something else or decided to upgrade.

Despite my restraint, it's amazing how you can become quite blasé about spending that sort of cash. I found myself saying things like, 'Well, I've only spent £19k on flowers, so

I'm under budget!' It gets to the point where the money stops being money, it's just numbers on a spreadsheet. And as long as the amount you've spent is less than the maximum amount you are allowed to spend, then that's fine!

When Matilda and Richard's big day arrived, their whopping budget did ensure some very special touches – including a videographer who set up a *Big Brother*-style 'diary room' where guests were able to leave messages that would be cut into the wedding video, instead of writing in a traditional guest book. They also had a range of spectacular cakes with different-flavoured layers that made an amazing five-tiered centrepiece; a pack of au pairs; and entertainers who'd give the children present a fabulous party of their own.

Best of all, the groom had taken 'sabrage' lessons and wowed the guests by slicing the top off the first bottle of champagne with a sword. (He'd seen it on TV once and thought this would be his only chance to give it a go!)

Even with all the fancy favours and flowers that money can buy, however, the real secret ingredients for a perfect wedding come from the guests and the atmosphere. Surprisingly enough, the memorable 'perfect' weddings that stick in my mind weren't the £100,000 ones. If you've got a bit of time on your hands, you can not only save money but incorporate some lovely personal touches.

I oversaw one beautiful country-themed wedding where almost everything was lovingly home-made.

The bride, Kerry, her mum and her sisters had picked all

the ivy to decorate the church, and in the build-up to the wedding they'd scoured charity shops for vintage-patterned duvet covers, which they then cut up to make bunting. Kerry had also saved jam jars, coffee jars and even pasta-sauce jars for a whole year, and she decorated them with ribbon and filled them with seasonal flowers to place on each table at her village-hall reception.

She arranged for there to be bales of hay outside the hall for people to sit on during the reception, and for entertainment she'd set up a coconut shy.

She didn't pay for bottled water, instead asking the caterers to put out jugs of tap water, but with ice cubes which had little flowers frozen inside. Also, instead of having the caterers serve a three-course meal, Kerry asked her friends to bring a pudding. Not only did her friends do her proud, they also looked so chuffed when their home-made delights were wolfed down by the guests.

The whole wedding was brilliant, with a really lovely atmosphere – proving that it's not about spending money; it's about spending time to make everything special and personal.

There are plenty of ways I've seen couples chop hundreds off their budgets by doing simple things like asking a friend to make their stationery, borrowing their wedding car from a friend or designating half a bottle of wine per head instead of going crazy with an unlimited bar.

How to Have a Beautiful Wedding on a Budget

- At the start, sit down and agree on what your absolute priorities are. The likelihood is that you probably can't afford to have the best of everything. So focus on your must-haves first.

- Once you've worked out your budget, you should aim to spend at least 10 per cent less. You will need this leeway, as extra costs always crop up. If the photographer suddenly costs £100, then it won't be a massive problem.

- Avoid the wedding forums! They're crazy, with everyone busy discussing things and getting very worked up. All it does is make brides really stressed and worried that their wedding isn't good enough.

- Don't be afraid to ask questions of suppliers. It will ensure that you find out about what's in the small print early on. There is nothing more frustrating than discovering, for example, that the photographer has an assistant who will also need feeding, and their travel costs paid.

- Avoid impulse spends, as that's where a lot of people go over budget – only to leave their extra buys in a box, unused. The amount of times a bride has come to me with a crazy look in her eye saying, 'I saw this and I love it!' And when you ask, 'How are you going to use it?', she'll say, 'I'll find a way!' The trick is to wait two weeks before you buy anything. Then, once the red dust has settled, if you can still justify spending the money and how you will use whatever it is you are buying, then go for it.

- The internet is a killer. It's amazing how quickly you can end up bidding on eBay for something you don't need. There'll be an offer for disposable cameras in bulk, ribbon for £20 a roll and cards for everyone in the bridal party. You just keep finding stuff, and then there are so many forums where other brides are talking. You click on a link and immediately decide: 'I should have that too!'

- Try getting married during the week, and reap the rewards of mid-week discounts. As one bride, Susie, says, 'Our Wednesday wedding meant that most people took the Tuesday and the Thursday off work. It meant we could all go to the local pub the night before, and we had a barbecue the day after. It made it a real event.'

• Contrary to popular belief, sticking to a budget is sensible rather than stingy, and even some celebrities know how to keep things modest at their weddings. Take Kate Winslet, who at her first wedding served her guests sausages and mash, or Natasha Kaplinsky, who went frugal and environmentally friendly by serving guests tap water rather than expensive bottled water. So, when even the celebs are realizing that huge and slightly indecent wedding budgets aren't the way to go, perhaps it's time the rest of us caught up.

One of the most difficult issues that would crop up when I was doing the full planning was how bride after bride expected me to help them eclipse the previous weddings they'd attended. This was particularly awkward when the ceremony the bride was hell-bent on beating was another one I'd masterminded.

Take Louise, who was introduced to me after I'd overseen her friend Anna's wedding. At our first meeting, it was clear that Louise had one objective in mind – to upstage Anna. To every question, she'd answer, 'What did Anna have? I want that but better . . .'

I'd really liked Anna, so I found the whole thing quite odd – not least when Louise started to make derogatory comments about her friend's taste.

'Don't you think Anna's table centres were a bit tacky?'

I was amazed. 'No,' I answered. 'Personally, I think they complemented the wedding theme.'

One thing's for sure, Louise wasn't one of my more likable brides. Come her wedding day, she spent quite a lot of her time fishing for compliments from her guests.

'Don't you just love this?' she'd say, gesturing towards a tiny detail, and then she'd scrutinize the victim's face to make sure that their reaction was suitably enthusiastic.

Louise's wedding was lovely, I can't deny it, but it wasn't necessarily better than anyone else's. And did it really matter if it was? As long as it was her dream day, surely that should be all that mattered?

Keen to keep on top of my game, I was now spending a lot of time studying US wedding websites and getting hold of imported US wedding magazines. A lot of British wedding crazes come over from the States, so I'd look for upcoming trends and then find good suppliers for them so I would know where to find them when the time came. By constantly expanding my list of suppliers, I could suggest services that suited my clients' needs, and it prevented my portfolio of weddings from seeming 'copycat', which can happen when you use the same suppliers over and over again.

The hard work paid off, and 2006 also brought with it an influx of exciting celebrity weddings.

When a famous star couple first signed me up to plan their wedding, I couldn't believe it. I was in my element. Flicking through the pages of *Heat* or *Hello!* in the past, I'd never thought in my wildest dreams that I'd end up planning weddings for the famous faces that featured in them. Now, here I was in the midst of the glitz and glamour, with massive budgets to play with.

Although that first celeb contract was very nerve-wracking, I kept reminding myself that it was 'just another wedding', and there was no more reason why this should go wrong simply because celebs were involved.

I've never been a star-struck person, and Mum's 'Treat others as you would wish to be treated' mantra has stood me in good stead, I think, but still it was very bizarre that Saturday to walk into a room and see those strangely familiar people wandering around in front of me.

As it happened, this particular famous couple wanted a very down-to-earth wedding, so it was really just the guests that were different!

Despite my thinking that first celebrity wedding was 'just another wedding', I soon came to realise that they were completely different from a normal wedding. You have a bride and a groom, but that's where the similarities end – especially when exclusive magazine deals come into play.

At a normal wedding, I'd have to make sure the photographer got a plate of sandwiches and a cup of tea, but at a wedding that had been bought up by a magazine, I'd find

I suddenly had twenty-five security guards to feed as well.

These smartly dressed men with earpieces (and the ability to cripple you with one thumb) would come armed with full guest lists, complete with photos, and vet women, men and children to ensure no gatecrashers had slipped through. To protect exclusivity, guests would be fleeced of all cameras and mobile phones, which would be deposited straight into the 'Guest Belonging' box, to be collected at the end of the day.

Unfortunately, the minute the rights to exclusive photos are sold, you are at the complete mercy of what the magazine wants and in danger of losing the atmosphere. Suddenly, beloved Grandma Kennedy and the rest of the clan are being seated at the back of the room where they can't be seen. Meanwhile, half a dozen soap stars, a crude comedian famed for his inappropriate quips and a bird who once flashed her boobs on *Big Brother* take pride of place near the top table – all because the photographer needs to snap them guffawing at the speeches and smiling lovingly at the bride (even if they've only met her once backstage at a TV chat show).

While most wedding photo sessions drag on, the celebrity ones are something else. Standard procedure is for the 'civilian' guests, who have already worked themselves up into an excited frenzy about the celebrities, to be shunted off and plied with alcohol at a four-hour reception. Then all the 'stars' are rounded up for the money shots. Hair and make-up is reapplied, and the stars are carefully guided into place for 'spontaneous' throwing-of-the-bouquet snaps. See, at celeb weddings, it's only other celebs that can get involved. Suddenly, it's more important to get the bride and groom posing next to Katie Price and her latest boyfriend rather than next to their proud parents.

When the reception begins, all the everyday guests end up rubber-necking to see what the stars are doing. Imagine trying to party and be natural about it while handfuls of well-known faces are in the room with you.

I'd always feel sorry for the normal guests, who'd suddenly start tugging at their off-the-peg dresses and shifting self-consciously in their New Look shoes, clearly uncomfortable that they were not nearly as skinny, tanned or groomed as the Armani-clad celebrities.

While a normal wedding might have a little box of chocolates on the table as favours, celebrity weddings tend to be much more lavish, and it's not unusual to have goodie bags to give away to guests at the end of the evening. These are often filled with freebies that the star's PR or the magazine has managed to organize: half-bottles of champagne, beauty products, make-up and chocolates – and, in one case, a voucher entitling all the guests to a night's stay at a five-star hotel.

Of course, once everyone has had a few drinks, the atmosphere begins to change. After the best part of a bottle of champagne, those star-struck guests are totally running on Dutch courage and can be seen sidling up to the celebrities to ask them to sign something. It's sweet if the celebrity is happy to play ball, but excruciating if they are rude.

I remember one surly ex-soap star who shot daggers at another guest who dared to smile at her from another table. Later in the day, she was clearly left mortified when the bride introduced her to the woman she'd snubbed – a TV executive. Having struggled to get paid acting work in the past few years, now Little Miss Surly was all sweetness and light. It was all very transparent, and the devil inside me couldn't help having a little chuckle.

When the magazine photos are over, and without their manager or PR to remind them of what they should and shouldn't do, I've seen a few celebs transform into their true chav selves. They can become very loud and screechy, having heated discussions with each other or throwing their heads back with a whoosh of blonde hair extensions and a blast of cackling laughter. Then when everyone hits the disco after the first dance, their inner exhibitionist comes out with abandon. There's pouting and hair flicking galore as they start bumping and grinding like they're in a Kanye West video – and this is normally done in front of an elderly aunt and uncle who are happily waltzing around the dancefloor and now don't know where to look.

Even the celeb guys can't resist pogoing up and down on the dancefloor with their mates after a few too many. It seems like it's in the male genes, whether you are a household name or not!

With a growing portfolio of celebrity nuptials under my belt, I was keen to keep the business growing, and my next big plan was to bring out a wedding book.

It started off as a bit of a pipe dream – I looked up how to write a proposal on the internet and sent it through to a few literary agents, not thinking I'd get very far. But one took me on, and then, as luck would have it, a publisher we approached said they were already looking to produce a 'How to . . .' guide to weddings and asked if I'd like to do it. My brief was to put together a guide that would show you how to have a fabulous wedding without getting sucked into all the expensive and unnecessary glitz.

While it was all very exciting, writing a book on top of running the business was no easy feat. It took me three months to complete, and to make it even more stressful, I was writing it from June until October – during the peak wedding period. Any plans to snuggle up for an early night with Michael went out the window as I sat at my laptop until the early hours of the morning.

Still, when my editor emailed to say she'd like to call it 'Tamryn Kirby's Wedding Secrets', I was bowled over.

I'll never forget the rush of wandering into Waterstone's and seeing a copy on the shelves for the first time. Sometimes, if it was tucked away, I'd take it off the shelf and replace it in a more prominent position. Apologies to the staff at the Waterstone's store in Reading if your displays were often disrupted. I confess!

We also sold the book through our website and, really sweetly, people would ask me to write little dedications inside. I was so touched.

I suspect one guy might even have used it to propose to

his girlfriend, as he asked me to write, 'Sarah, you might need this . . . best wishes, Tamryn.' Aww.

Spurred on by the success of the book deal, I then decided to approach Debenhams. Debenhams had one of the most complete wedding services offered on the high street, doing everything from stationery and suits to gowns and gift lists, and I thought their customers might be exactly the type who would go for our 'on-the-day' service, so I emailed the wedding brand manager and also his business development counterpart and told them all about my business.

'We could come in and consult with you,' I said. 'We know what brides want.'

I didn't really expect to hear back, so it was a real surprise when they called to invite me in for a meeting. It took place at the Debenhams head office in Welbeck Street. Any nerves I might have had soon evaporated when I was met by Alex, the brand manager, a very smiley chap who reminded me ever so slightly of my dad, and Paul, the business development manager, who was younger and sharper with a great sense of humour.

'We're really impressed by what you've sent us,' Alex told me. 'How would you feel about getting involved in our wedding stationery range and endorsing it? We could feature you in the brochure and you could give some hints and tips.'

Well, I nearly fell off my chair. It took all the skills I'd picked up at weddings about keeping calm when you get a shock to stop me shrieking with excitement.

'Perhaps you can do some presentations in our stores as well,' Paul added.

'Um, I'd love to,' I managed to splutter.

It was mind-blowing, but they seemed to be really embracing TK Weddings – even inviting me to be on their huge stand at the National Wedding Show. I was absolutely blown away, and after the meeting I spent the entire taxi journey back to Paddington completely dazed and grinning like crazy.

Now, I'm a girl who has more notebooks, pads and greetings cards than you can shake a stick at. I love stationery and, quite sadly, I love the thrill of writing on the first empty page in a new journal. So, as you can imagine, the task of working with the wedding stationery manager was one I absolutely adored.

Suddenly I was being sent glorious boxes of samples for my new range. It was then my job to give my opinion regarding the design, colour schemes, alterations and embellishments. After marvelling at beautiful invitations decorated with silk ribbon and lace, I'd write a few lines about which invitations from the range would suit which wedding style for the catalogue. It was a huge buzz and, on top of that, my company was promoted in the brochure as well. How lucky was I?

5.

Bridezillas and
Serene Brides

It was as the guests filed out of the country house behind the bride and groom that I noticed the poor guy slumped on the floor near the back of the room.

He was clearly in the midst of an epileptic fit, and his wife was kneeling on the floor trying to put her coat under his head.

As I rushed over to help, his fit began to subside, so I helped his wife to put him in the recovery position and then called for an ambulance.

Concerned that the bride and groom might get a start from the impending sound of sirens, I briefly excused myself, heading outside to find them. The groom was in the middle of having a photo taken with all his ushers, so I quickly asked the bride for a quiet word. I felt guilty about telling her but figured it would be better to warn her before she was confronted with the sight of an ambulance screeching to a halt outside the house.

'I know I promised to assist with the photos, but one of your guests is a bit unwell,' I explained. I was just reassuring her that I was sure the gentleman would be fine when she interrupted me.

'I really don't care,' she sighed, with a dismissive wave of her hand. 'He wasn't someone I wanted to come anyway.' And with that she sauntered over to her husband and switched on the perfect smile and unruffled 'serene bride' persona. I had to laugh – sometimes, you just can't beat the sheer bloody single-mindedness of a bride on her wedding day. There she is, looking all dreamy and gorgeous, when actually the beast within is waiting, ready to unleash fire and fury on anything or anyone who gets in her way.

Although the Bridezilla is the type of hell-bent wife-to-be who it seems would have 'My day, my way' tattooed on her forehead, you can't always predict who has the monster gene. There are wives-to-be who are lovely, polite and adorable in the run-up. But just as you start to relax, something switches, and their true Jekyll and Hyde tendencies are unleashed. Just like a slasher movie, you have no way of seeing it coming. It's only when you turn up on the morning of the wedding, walk through the door and see the wild glint in the bride's eye that alarm bells start to ring. 'Oh God, here we go,' you think. Suddenly the whole serene bride thing is out the window, and you're faced with the sight of a petite blonde decked out in ivory satin stomping around and swearing like a sailor.

Yet, comically, after ranting and raving behind the scenes, head swivelling like something out of *The Exorcist*, the histrionics are over in a heartbeat the minute she steps out to meet 'her public'. With all eyes fixed on her, she quickly adopts the smug smile of an actress sauntering on to the stage to collect an Oscar. Quick as a flash, the grimaces are replaced by sweet smiles and she's gliding about like butter wouldn't melt, greeting her guests with little regal waves, air-kisses and coy little giggles.

I've met some astonishing Bridezillas in my time, but Sheila will always have a place in my heart as a particularly special one. In what can only be described as a week from hell, Jake was struck down by chicken pox just as I was gearing myself up for a wedding with one of my most testing brides.

As the Saturday approached, I had a real sinking feeling. I wanted to stay at home and look after my little boy, but as per usual I was committed, this week to Sheila and her fiancé Grant's wedding. Sheila was a career girl who worked in the City and hardly likely to sympathize with my plight, but with Jake sick and feverish on the Friday night, I suspected that, for once in my career, I might have to miss a wedding. But during a frantic phone round to all my staff, I was dismayed to find that no one was available to step in. There was nothing for it: I was going to have to abandon my sick son and go to work.

The next morning, I fought back tears as I tiptoed into Jake's bedroom to find him out for the count in a feverish sleep, horrid red marks covering every inch of his skin.

'I'll try and get away a bit early,' I promised Michael.

'Sure,' he replied. I couldn't help but notice the resentment in his voice.

Arriving at the wedding venue, I was dismayed to find my not-so-radiant bride caterwauling at an innocent chambermaid. Apparently, Sheila the Diva had expressly asked for extra towels in her bathroom. How was she supposed to get ready for her wedding without them?

'You idiot,' she spat at the young girl, before finishing her tirade with a line guaranteed to set my Bridezilla radar on full alert: 'I'm the *bride* and if *my* day is ruined because of *you*, I'll have you *sacked*!'

As the terrified girl scurried out of the room, I braced myself, ready for the moment Sheila would turn on me. But instead, rather disarmingly, she embraced me in a hug (not too tight, in case I disturbed her spectacular up-do) and indulged me with three air-kisses.

'Tamryn,' she said in a singsong voice. 'Thank *goodness* you're here. You're the only one I can trust.'

'Heaven help me,' I thought. 'I've got a right one here.'

I could see all the danger signs. If I was the only person she could trust, there was one thing I could look forward to for the rest of the day, and that was taking the blame – for everything.

At the same time, I was on tenterhooks about Jake, trying my hardest to smile and do a good job but hating myself for being such a bad mother. It felt like everything I'd worked so hard for was unravelling and as if all my priorities were wrong. I was expanding my business to build up a secure future for my son, but was I neglecting him in the process?

To make matters worse, Michael didn't seem to be

coping all that well. The flurry of texts just kept on coming.

'The spots are worse . . .'

'His eyes are closing up . . .'

'He's really hot, what do I do?'

Back at the wedding, Sheila appeared to be loving her moment. As she floated from guest to guest working her 'beautiful bride' moment, I had a brief hope that the histrionics were over. But then, just before a group photo with the entire wedding party, I saw her beckoning to me with a determined look on her face. 'Oh God, here we go,' I thought.

'Tamryn,' she hissed in my ear. 'You have to go and speak to *that* guest in the purple dress. Go and tell her to turn her engagement ring round for the photos. It's bigger than *mine*.'

I stood there for a minute, waiting for the peals of laughter that would confirm it was all a big joke. But instead Sheila just eyeballed me with a look that said, 'Why are you still here?' Then she turned her back on me to morph magically into the perfect bride.

Heavy-footed, I began to walk across the grass towards the guest in question. 'Oh God, I'm actually going to do this,' I thought to myself.

Arriving in front of the purple-dressed blinger, I bit my lip and cleared my throat.

'Err, the bride has asked if you could hide your ring for the photos,' I stammered, trying to smile, like it was the most reasonable request in the world.

'What?' Miss Purple replied, glancing towards the bride.

'You cannot be serious?' My deadpan face confirmed that I absolutely was.

I soon realized I was getting daggers from all angles. The bride was looking at me like I was a piece of shit and now so was the guest. 'Yep, you're wasting your time,' I thought. 'No one could possibly make me feel any more of a sap . . .'

With Jake being ill as well, it was all too much. Locking myself in a toilet cubicle and slumping on the seat, I put my head in my hands, trying to keep my sobs as quiet as possible. Then, as soon as the first dance was over, I made my excuses and raced home to my son.

A few weeks later, I found myself facing humiliation once more, when I was forced to circulate a ridiculous tall story for a bride. She wanted me to tell everyone that the reason her dress was bulging at the seams was because of a food allergy. In actual fact, Gina had squeezed herself into a wedding dress that was at least a size too small.

Every bride wants to look amazing on her wedding day, and many get there sensibly, through healthy eating, cutting down on alcohol, early nights and exercise. But others choose the alternative route. They're so desperate to be a size eight when they walk up the aisle, they don't care if this almost puts them in hospital.

Hair extensions, nail extensions, fake tans and colonic irrigation are just the tip of the iceberg, as brides who want to create an unbelievable day strive to make themselves absolutely unbelievable – to the point where some grooms don't actually recognize the woman standing at the end of the aisle!

Then there's the big one – the dress. I've seen some very plain women utterly transformed by the perfect wedding dress. Sadly, I've also seen the opposite, as was the case with Gina.

OK, so we're all prone to it. Like all women, I've convinced myself that I can wear in the shoes that are actually a size too small, or that the ill-fitting top I'm not sure about will somehow look amazing once I get it home and manage to accessorize it suitably. But the £1,000 dress you purchase for your wedding day? Take it from me: you will not fool anyone and, even worse, there will be photographic evidence.

A dress that is too small will only ever look bad, while the right size could look lovely. It is impossible to hold your tummy in for an entire wedding day and, in any case, who really wants to attempt that feat on the most photographed day of her life? If you lose weight, you can always get your dress taken in. Don't set yourself an unachieveable goal.

Unfortunately, there was no reasoning with Gina. She'd bought a size-eight dress, and she was going to fit into it at all costs.

It was a worthy effort, and you had to admire her commitment. She hit the gym with a vengeance and endured quite a period of fasting, but still she wasn't quite skinny enough. I suspect she'd never been a size eight in her life, and the fact was, no matter how much she abstained, her natural frame was never going to be any smaller than a size ten. Even the wraps and colonic irrigation couldn't shift those last stubborn pounds.

On the morning of her wedding, I found myself staring at the floor as two bridesmaids worked up a sweat desperately trying to squeeze her into her dress. Even with a waist-cinching corset and the most punishing magic pants, it was still a struggle.

Eventually the gown was heaved into place, but it was so tight that the poor woman looked mummified, and the lace-up bit at the back just couldn't be pulled tight. Even worse, she was now sporting 'back boobs' – unsightly rolls of flesh hung over the back of her dress.

When she saw herself in the mirror she balked at her reflection and I could see she was close to tears – as could the photographer, who suddenly stopped snapping the 'informal bride getting ready' pics and shuffled awkwardly out of the room.

'Oh God,' Gina whimpered. 'Tamryn, you have to come up with a story. Just tell everyone I'm allergic to wheat or something.'

So yet again I found myself doing the walk of shame around the wedding, bleating off a story with absolutely no conviction because I was too soft to do anything else.

'Oh, Gina's had a bit of a trying morning,' I found myself announcing to a bunch of her old uni friends. 'She had something in her breakfast that doesn't agree with her and she's got a bloated tummy.'

Yep, and we've flown the Pope in from Rome to marry them too . . . Who on earth was I trying to kid? I'm sure I saw a few eyebrows raised.

Poor Gina, not only did the dress look wrong but it

clearly was a struggle to wear as well. She spent the entire day breathing shallowly and was obviously in a great deal of discomfort. Then when there was a slight ripping sound as her groom helped her sit down on her chair. I prayed to God it wasn't what I thought it was.

You've guessed it – her dress had ripped from the strain, and was now gaping under the armpit. I managed to truss her up in the toilets with some masking tape, but it could have all been so easily avoided.

At the end of the day, you simply have to be realistic. Nobody but you is going to know what size the dress is and, trust me, after the sheer number of them I've seen, you'll always look better in a well-fitting size twelve than an overly optimistic size eight that shows every little bulge or doesn't even zip up. The last thing you want is to be strapped into a torture device all day and be so distracted that the only thing you remember about your own wedding is your eternal struggle for breath.

I'll never forget one bride, who'd opted for an overtly sexy wedding dress and lived to pay the consequences.

Nicky was quite a busty girl and had gone for a strapless dress. It was all a bit Kerry Katona – a lot of boob all round, and also the common curse of back boobs where she was laced in so tightly. Never a good look, especially not on your wedding day.

It was while she was dancing, jumping up and down, that the unthinkable happened. A heaving breast made an impromptu appearance, popping out of her dress. It took a minute or two for her to realize – by which time the majority of the guests around her had already copped an eyeful. Thankfully, she chose to laugh it off, so people didn't take it too seriously. At least it didn't happen during her first dance.

Then there was poor Sadie, another bride I heard about, who only discovered that her dress wasn't ready the night before the wedding. She called me in a complete panic: somehow, the dressmaker had managed to damage the fabric on the bodice. Even worse, the straps of the dress had been placed on with poppers to save the dressmaker time, but being in the wrong place, they sprung off every time she moved. In the end she ripped them off theatrically during dinner, which got a big laugh.

Although it was annoying, Sadie managed to keep her perspective on things and later claimed that it hadn't marred her day.

'I was on such a high about getting married that nothing else mattered,' she said.

How to Avoid Wedding-dress Weeping . . .

- Have a final fitting at least a month in advance to iron out any issues and, during it, make sure you practise all the moves you will make on the day. Stand, walk, sit, kneel and throw an imaginary bouquet.

- Everyone wants to look beautiful, but it's worth being a little bit practical as well. I had to feel for the bride who decided on a medieval-style dress with huge draping sleeves. They dragged along the floor all day and got coated in food. Not a good look.

- If you're having a church wedding, remember to be reserved. Don't end up like the bride who chose a sleek halterneck dress scooped down to the small of her back and was asked by the vicar to cover up during the service. If you want to go sexy, then opt for a pretty wrap or faux fur stole to cover up with during the church service. That way, when you take it off at the reception, you'll have a bigger impact.

- A duvet cover is the best thing to keep your dress in – it's big enough to avoid the dress becoming creased at the bottom, and cotton is breathable so your dress will stay super-fresh, without any lingering odour of plastic.

- If you've got an impressive train on your dress, don't forget to speak to your dress supplier to make sure you've got a 'loop' sewn in – this means you can tie your train up in the evening so that you can hit the dancefloor with no worries about tripping or slipping.

- Lacing on the back of a dress can take a while to do, and it can take a bit of practice to get right. It's worth having a trial run with whoever is going to be strapping you in on the day.

One of the big expenses for a bride is her dress – they can often cost an extortionate amount.

I, personally, can't think of any occasion where I'd willingly spend £2,000 on a dress – especially one that only gets worn for eight hours. Yet time and time again I've seen brides telling themselves their dress is 'a steal', because it only cost £2,500 when they set their dress budget at £3,000.

If you look around, there are great dress agencies out there where you can pick up a really good bargain. These dresses might be second-hand, but having been lovingly cleaned, updated or repaired, you'd never know. Putting them on, you'd assume they were brand-new. I know one bride who picked up the most beautiful dress from Oxfam. She had it altered and added sequins and stones, and it saved her an absolute fortune.

If you really have your heart set on something completely new, a lot of bridal shops sell off dresses for a reduced price at the end of the season, so that's really worth considering.

I do think, though, you should be careful of eBay, as the chances are your dress is being shipped from somewhere in the Far East, and if there is a problem with it, it could be a struggle to send it back.

Even if a dress is delivered in perfect condition, you have to take care to keep it that way. I always find it amazing that some brides don't take better care of their dresses. I've arrived on wedding mornings to find dresses in a very sorry state, after having been rolled up and shoved in a suitcase.

Another thing is that, even if you do look after your dress, it is hardly the most practical of outfits, and many brides make the mistake of thinking they can keep their beloved frock perfect and flawless until the end of the day. Unfortunately, the reality is that your big white dress is likely to attract dirt, gunk, wine and food with almost magnetic force.

One of my brides even had her wedding train reversed over by her wedding car. Just before her church entrance, there she was with a dirty black tyre mark across the back of her dress. I'd expected an instant hissy fit, a torrent of abuse and tears, and possible GBH committed on the unwitting driver who did the deed. But as I tried to appease her, assuring her that we could chalk over the mark or edit it out of the photos with computer wizardry, the bride put a hand on my arm.

'Tamryn, is he here?' she asked, nodding towards the church.

'Yes,' I replied.

'Well,' she smiled, 'that's the only thing that matters.' And away she went to marry her man.

If you do decide you want to avoid frock horrors, then there is always the choice not to go for a traditional white meringue. A couple of brides I know opted for scarlet and burgundy dresses to mark their winter weddings. Another bride, who had beautiful curly hair, looked stunning in a white trouser suit that she'd accessorized with lovely shoes and a big necklace. As her new husband said in his speech, 'I never expected Tash to wear anything other than this, and she looks beautiful.' Lovely.

And one newlywed changed into a little fifties-style knee-length dress – with a tight bust and layered skirt with netting – after the meal. It meant she could dance to her heart's content without having to worry about a heavy skirt and train restricting her – plus she had a back-up dress, something another bride, Eva, would have given her right arm for . . .

In Eva's own personal frocky horror story, I could only watch in alarm from a distance as she leaned forward to hug her friend and somehow managed to smear tomato soup down her bodice. She looked like she'd been stabbed, and there was no hope of doing anything to reduce the bright-red stain.

Whereas some brides would have been reduced to tears, Eva actually took it very good-naturedly. Sighing at the state of her dress, she simply shrugged and said, 'Well, thank God the photos are over.'

I loved her for her reaction, and as we stood in the toilets trying to clean things up a little, I was amazed to see her laughing at her own misfortune. She was a very level-headed, lovely bride.

Sometimes, watching the most calm, relaxed girls degenerate into forehead-gripping, perma-scowled stress-heads, I wondered just what powerful properties that engagement ring wields. This shiny little object is supposed to be a symbol of joy and lifetime union, so why was I watching it suck out all the bride's life force, as happens to Frodo in *Lord of the Rings*, and fast-propelling her into marriage Mordor?

I think there is a mistaken view these days that wedding stress is a bridal must-have. You only have to log on to any wedding forum and head for any post entitled 'emotional support' to see how brides love to whip themselves up into a total frenzy. If you weren't stressed before, then don't worry: 'princessB2B' (the B2B stands for bride-to-be – oh yes, it's a whole different language out there) will tell you exactly why you *soooo* should be.

Similarly, it always amazes me that some wedding-insurance companies actually offer couples pre-wedding stress counselling as part of the package. Talk about tempting fate. Perhaps, instead, there should be discounts for clients who keep a constant blood pressure while planning their wedding.

Interestingly, the brides who spend their entire lives telling people what a 'nightmare' their wedding is becoming are often the very same girls who'd announce to me: 'I'd *love* to have your job.' I'd just think, 'Really? I'm juggling seventeen weddings at the moment, yet you have one and you're drinking bottles of Rescue® Remedy like Panda Pop.'

Of course planning a wedding can be difficult. When people don't live near their families and can't ask for help, when things aren't going to plan and there are politics and fall-outs to deal with, it is hard.

But 'I'm planning a wedding therefore I've got to be stressed' is not the way it has to be. If you do spend every waking moment obsessing about your wedding, then it's not surprising to find yourself slowly slipping into Bridezilla-dom. If it's all you think about, it will be all you talk about, and then the fact that your invitations are a slightly different shade of cream to the one you asked for becomes a life and death issue.

The Bride Guide

The Wannabe

Will only use suppliers who've worked with celebs, and wants J-Lo's cake designer. Only a Vera Wang dress will do, and Tiffany jewellery is a must. She wants to know if you can invite any celebrities for her.

Most likely to say: 'But I saw this in *Hello!* magazine!'

Mummy's Little Treasure

Her mother comes to every meeting and holds court while she sits meekly, apparently mute. She's going to wear Mummy's wedding dress, even though it looks like a sack of spuds on her.

Most likely to say: 'I don't think Mummy would like that.'

The Control Freak

Carries her wedding file everywhere with her and is obsessed with her 'to do' list. She has her suppliers on speed-dial on her BlackBerry. Everyone is given a minute-by-minute schedule for the day.

Most likely to say: 'This wasn't in my plan!' while gripping her forehead tightly.

The Breakdown Bride

She arrives at every wedding-related meeting with a wobbling bottom lip and a pack of tissues. She thinks everyone is conspiring against her and that she's doomed to have a disastrous day. She always has her mum flapping with her, as she can't make any decisions on her own.

Most likely to say: 'I just can't cope with this any more!'

Robo-bride

Loses friends along the way and is liable to make suppliers cry with her ridiculous demands. She will get what she wants come hell or high water, and no one is getting in her way, not even the groom.

Most likely to say: 'I don't care if you're already booked, you're still doing *my* wedding.'

The Smiling Assassin

In the run-up to the wedding, she's absolutely fine — lovely, in fact. But then, on her wedding day, the red mist descends, and suddenly she's stomping around screaming at everyone like Janice Dickinson.

Most likely to say: 'Get out of my way, I'm the fucking bride!'

The Starvation Queen

This usually comes as an emergency reaction to a bride not fitting into her dress or thinking she looks a bit big in pre-wedding photos. She spends the two months leading up to the wedding living on a diet of apples and lettuce leaves. She is permanently stroppy due to hunger and looks like she's going to faint.

Most likely to say: 'No, really, I'm not hungry,' while eyeing your bagel with a crazed look.

Bootcamp Bride

Dreams of being honed and toned for the photos but becomes so obsessed you can practically see her six-pack through the dress. This lady gets up at 5.30 every morning and has a photo of Madonna's arms on her fridge.

Most likely to say: 'Just another hundred sit-ups for today. Is there a gym at the wedding venue?'

Plastic Princess

Fake tan and fake nails are just the start with this bride. Next she's opting for teeth-whitening and ear-pinning (because she wanted an up-do). Likewise, Botox and liposuction are treated as casually as facials are for the majority of brides.

Most likely to say: 'Shall I put my surgeon on the top table?'

Miss Serene

She's very smiley, very normal and keeps everything in perspective. Suppliers love her and would do anything for her. She doesn't make mountains out of molehills and consequently everything goes her way.

Most likely to say: 'As long as I marry him, nothing else matters.'

I, of course, could have done with some of my own advice!

As my company became more and more successful, it was true that I, too, had become tunnel-visioned. I let my interests and hobbies slip. It's hard not to when your job is so all-encompassing.

We'd just had a series on Discovery TV called *The Wedding Planners*, where the TV company had followed me and some of the other girls around to meetings, weddings, and to visit suppliers. Filming took up a lot of time and, looking back, I don't think it was necessarily an accurate representation of us or the job, but it certainly didn't hurt the business. The web stats after the show would go through the roof.

With another deluge of clients I took on three more members of staff: Naomi, a dark, serious-looking girl who surprised everyone with her filthy laugh and was based in Essex; Claire, who was in Yorkshire, completely down-to-earth and brilliant; and red-headed Rosie, a beautiful girl from Sussex who had a knack of remembering every little detail.

Despite taking on more staff, though, I still had to co-ordinate everything, and I was continually aware that, when you work for yourself, the buck stops with you.

In theory, I worked three days a week while Jake went to nursery, but in reality, once the wedding planning took off, no point of my week was work-free. Most of my clients worked during the week, and therefore they'd want to deal with their planner out of work hours. I'd regularly find myself inundated with calls and emails on evenings and weekends.

I knew I shouldn't get into the habit of replying straight away, but I also knew that if I didn't do it there and then, there would soon be a backlog, and that impatient brides would be less than impressed by what they'd view as a 'slack' response. After all, I was their wedding planner, and surely their wedding is the most important one I was dealing with?

On the days when Jake wasn't in nursery or, later, at school, I felt really torn. I wanted to spend time with him on my 'days off', but often I'd have to do little tasks and projects at the same time – some of which rubbed off on him. Hence Jake was the only child I knew under five who knew which order wine glasses were placed on a table!

But as work got busier and busier, I began to feel like I was missing out on a lot of key moments in Jake's life. Often it would be Michael taking Jake to his friend's birthday party, because I was running around after yet another bride.

Then, once Jake went to school, it got even harder, as I was often working weekends and missing out on precious time with him.

Although my hours were fairly flexible during the week, which meant I could shift a few things round to attend a parents' evening or a school concert, the same couldn't be said for weekends.

One Saturday, when Jake had a special school picnic, I

was mortified to face the wrath of a stroppy four-year-old the following day. 'All the other mummies were there, and I was just with Daddy,' he told me. 'I wanted *you* there.'

Although I managed to appease him by promising to take him to the zoo, my 'bad mother' conscience wasn't so easily pacified.

At least I knew that, on the whole, things with Jake were great. He was older now, more able to communicate, and easy to look after. As long as you stuck to his routine, he was a very even-tempered child, who never had tantrums in supermarkets and could always be trusted to behave when I took him out.

But on our days together, I was balancing looking after him and doing things with him with dealing with phone calls and emails from clients. Sometimes, getting Jake into bed at the end of a long day was no form of relief, because I knew I would have messages to reply to, problems to solve and business admin to handle.

Looking back, I hate myself for putting other people before my son, but at the time, I think I was so scared about losing my business – possibly the only thing that was keeping me going – that I did it unquestioningly.

And it wasn't just my family that was suffering. My dedication to wedding planning was also playing havoc with my social life.

Impromptu nights out with friends or grabbing a quick coffee or lunch soon went out of the window as I became more and more booked up. My friends understood that it was my job, but I began to feel as if I was always letting people down. I was fast becoming 'boring Tamryn', who never did anything but work.

The one thing that saved me was that, every Wednesday, without fail, I'd meet up with Debs and Julie for a glass of wine, and it was them I would confide in about my worries about Michael.

If I'm honest about it, it felt like I was living a split life. Professionally, things were wonderful, and building my business had given me back the strength and confidence I'd lost – but I was well aware that sacrifices were being made. Michael and I barely spent any 'quality' time together. With both of us working so hard, we hardly ever had a night out or did anything together. Our main issue was a complete lack of communication, and it ran deep: I didn't like asking for help, and Michael didn't know how to offer it.

I felt like I was trying to do two things – run a business and be a mum and housewife – while Michael could just come and go with his work, knowing that I'd always be at home to look after Jake.

Despite the success I was having, I never felt that I was taken seriously as a businesswoman or that my achievements were appreciated or understood. Michael probably felt that I was more wrapped up in my business than in him, and neither of us seemed to know what to do to make the situation better.

Debs and Julie would listen patiently then offer their advice, which was that, somehow, we had to find some quality time together.

Determined to reignite the spark, I planned and prepared special meals for when Michael came home from work. I lit the table with candles and tried to engage him in conversation, but even when he tried to smile and ask me questions in reply, it all seemed a bit stilted. I didn't know what to do, so I preferred not to think about it. Instead I ploughed on with work.

The transient friendships I had which saw me nurture fiancées into brides worked well for me. If my life was filled with breaking news on my clients' hopes, dreams and delights, then I didn't have to think about anything else.

So more than ever, I immersed myself in these intense six-month relationships, lapping up the lives of the brides I'd speak to on the phone every day. I enjoyed it, and knowing I was the first person on speed-dial when a bride bagged her perfect dress never failed to touch me.

While I enjoyed doing my best for the lovely brides who came my way, it was a slightly more strained exercise when it came to the nutty, smutty or bonkers ones. I never quite understood why they felt the need suddenly to divulge the most intimate details to me.

'I'm in a sex shop in Soho!' one bride cackled down the phone as I walked swiftly out of Jake's earshot. 'I'm getting crotchless knickers, handcuffs and a whip for my wedding night!'

Another candid bride decided to tell me all about her topiary plans – for her *lady* garden!

'Simon loves me hair-free,' she giggled (while I tried not

to gag). You try looking the groom in the eye when you know exactly what the bride has planned for his wedding night. I wasn't paid enough to be saddled with that kind of mental image, thank you very much.

Then there were the brides who announced their plans to cut off all carnal rights in the lead-up to the big day. You would not believe the number of women who suddenly decide on a period of celibacy before their big day, in the mistaken belief that it will 'spice things up' or somehow clear their conscience to wear white (or that more flattering-in-the-photos shade of ivory).

'I've told my husband we won't have sex for the three months before the wedding so when we do it'll be really special,' one girl chirped.

'No! Don't do it!' I wanted to yell. 'You're just ensuring that a whole load more stress and arguments will come your way.'

The simple fact is that if waiting until the wedding night was really that important, *you would have waited*. Not having sex for three months isn't going to turn you into a virgin bride again, no matter how much you want it to.

To be honest, planning that extra-special wedding night is rarely worth the bother. Take it from me, the number of newlyweds who actually have sex on their wedding night is a lot smaller than you'd think. After ten hours of stressing, eating and, of course, drinking, most people are far too tired or too drunk to bother. One of my brides even ended up passing out in her wedding dress, as she was just too exhausted to take it off. And with the amount of hooks, ties and strapping on the frocks, most grooms don't stand a chance of seductively undressing their brides – not without a crew of extras to help them anyway. So that's that romantic moment out of the window.

Either way, nobody needs to know whether you've consummated the marriage – especially not your wedding planner.

Anyway, I digress – back to the bonkers brides.

As well as the shameless sharing of too much information, there were the wailer brides. As soon as their names flashed up on my phone, I'd get a feeling of dread. In all likelihood, the next hour would be lost, as they tearfully poured out their souls to me:

'We're not having sex . . .'

'I'm so stressed . . .'

'I've never been this miserable . . .'

As they hyperventilated down the phone, I'd try calmly to help them see the light. Did they really want to live in a world where panic attacks and hysterical phone calls constituted their daily existence?

I'd advise them to take a moment and do the sanity check:

First, pretend it's not your wedding and you're actually a guest: would you ever have noticed that the curtains in the venue don't quite match (and be honest now). Then, think back to all the weddings you've been to and the things the bride said were a problem: did you spot them? Can you even remember? Probably not.

Overtly controlling and obsessed brides were the bane of my life. I could be having my only Saturday off in months, but that wouldn't register with the manic bride who wanted to call me at 8 a.m. to debate invitations. And, believe me, when a bride asks, 'How are you?' at the start of a phone conversation, she doesn't actually want to hear anything but, 'I'm fine, now let's talk about your wedding.'

Mind you, at least I was being paid to suffer, while the grooms were probably just completely bewildered by the dramatic change in the woman they fell in love with. As brides become completely engulfed by their plans, it's often their partner who takes the brunt of the madness. Grooms are bullied into wearing lots of pink, having dancing lessons and attending day-long flower-selection sessions.

Complaints along the lines of 'She's not the same person' are expressed again and again. 'We don't get any non-wedding weekends'; 'I found her wailing on the floor because the car she wanted to take her to the church is already booked.'

Then the bride will tell you, 'Something is not right. We're not doing stuff together.'

Of course the bride is always going to care about the little details, but the most important thing is to keep everything in perspective. The fact that the centrepieces are missing a ribbon pales in comparison to things like, for example, the vicar not turning up, so take a deep breath and try to go with the flow. Most people will only remember whether you looked happy or not, and if everyone had a great day.

Careful planning is one thing, but it's all too easy to go that step too far into complete and utter obsession. And that's not good for anyone!

I think a lot of brides fall into the trap of thinking they need to be superwoman, dealing with everything by themselves and not imposing on their husbands-to-be, but that's just not necessary.

I remember one bride who even had to be signed off sick from work for two weeks, because she couldn't eat or sleep and wouldn't stop crying over her wedding. Her GP diagnosed stress and banned all wedding talk for a fortnight. If it gets to that point, then something really needs to give.

Indeed, there have been a couple of occasions when I actually wondered if I was going to have to book separate rooms for the supposedly happy couple.

There's nothing worse than seeing newly-weds sniping at each other in front of the guests; everyone can recognize the narrowed eyes, stiff body language and the icy tone of voice. And all this from two people who've just committed to spending the rest of their lives together!

I remember one groom's speech where he said of his new bride, 'I'm so lucky – see how beautiful she looks!'

There was an audible gasp as the bride eyeballed him and replied, 'Well, that's not what you said two days ago!'

Real-life Bridezillas Confess All!

'I asked my wedding venue to redecorate the reception room so that it matched my colour scheme. When they refused, I asked them to at least turn the curtains round so the pattern wouldn't clash with my other decorations.'

'When my mother-in-law-to-be showed me the outfit that she'd bought for the wedding, I told her she'd have to take it back because it clashed with what the bridesmaids were wearing.'

'I was obsessed with my invitations – so much so that I drove around town posting a couple in each postbox in case one postbox was vandalized and all my invitations were in it.'

'My sister told me to grow my hair, stop colouring it and lose a stone and then I might be good enough to be a bridesmaid.'

'My husband-to-be and I drove 150 miles to a fabric factory to try and get the exact material I wanted for my bridesmaids' dresses, but when we got there, I didn't like any of them. My fiancé said I had to choose something, and I had a temper tantrum right in the factory in front of everyone.'

'I was sacked from my post of chief bridesmaid by my best friend after she went all Bridezilla – I told her I was pregnant and she said she didn't want a "fat woman waddling up the aisle". We've not spoken since.'

'At the end of the evening on my wedding day, my brother, after around a dozen too many drinks, decided to do a "little sister" speech over the microphone. Pretty tipsy myself, I immediately instructed one of my pals to show great admiration once he'd finished, because I was so embarrassed that he could barely speak – let alone string a sentence together. When she duly whooped at my request, I threw her a scowl and accused her of "laughing at my poor brother", before turning on my ivory heel. Needless to say, she was the first person I called the morning after to eat humble pie. She still talks about it now!'

If *I* felt like an agony aunt, then it must have been tenfold for these girls' poor friends – particularly the maid of honour.

If you're getting married, it's important to try not to bombard your friends with every tiny detail of the day and each and every little glitch. It's your wedding, after all, not theirs. Weddings are generally happy occasions which bring people together, so to lose a friend in the build-up would be a real tragedy.

Yet I did have one bitchy bride who actually 'sacked' her bridesmaid weeks before the wedding – all because she hadn't pandered to her every outrageous whim. Years of friendship were about to be thrown out of the window because of a condition I like to call Obsessive Bride Syndrome.

For the past six months, dear, demanding Donna had expected her oldest friend, Sasha, to be at her bridal beck and call. Sasha was required to be there for everything – and I mean everything! In a verbal assault both over the phone and in person, Donna had spent hours pouring her heart out to Sasha about every tiny detail of the wedding. She'd plied her best friend with a never-ending list of things to do and filled her diary with dates of dress fittings and wedding shows.

But Sasha had a full-time job and a life of her own – understandably, she just didn't want or need to be on constant stand-by to fulfil Donna's every wish and demand. I could tell things were getting a little tense and tried to be the peacekeeper but, sometimes, you know you're just fighting a losing battle.

I'd spend ages on the phone to Sasha, trying to persuade her to come along to the hundredth dress fitting, while she, quite reasonably, explained she had something urgent in her own life to do that day and couldn't make it. Minutes later, I'd find myself calling Donna, uttering platitudes and agreeing that it was all so very dreadful of her. I'd hang up feeling sycophantic and hating myself for encouraging Bridezilla behaviour but also knowing it was my job to keep the bride happy.

Soon, though, the emails, calls and stories about Sasha became more and more frequent until one day Donna phoned to declare she had now stripped her of *all* bridesmaid duties.

I assumed Donna would be sad to have fallen out so badly with her best friend, but when I phoned to check on her a couple of days later, she was disturbingly cold. Indeed her most pressing concerns were whether she could get her money back for Sasha's dress and which one of them all their friends were going to side with.

By the time the wedding day came around, almost everyone knew about the big fall-out, and the bride definitely hadn't come out of things well. As I heard her boast for the millionth time, 'Sasha's whole problem is jealousy, because she'll never find a bloke as great as mine,' it made me wince.

'You, my dear, are heading for a big fall,' I muttered under my breath, before reminding myself to smile sweetly.

And if it's not the best friend getting it in the neck, then it just might be the poor groom.

More than one confided to me that he had no idea how to calm his manic, stressed bride, and my advice to the pair of them would be to have a realistic talk about how to put it right again. If you no longer feel in control of your wedding, if it is causing you sleepless nights, then you need to find a way to step back and regain control. It's you who feeds the beast of wedding paranoia and panic, you and no one else.

Take the couple who booked me a year in advance for a massive wedding at a local cathedral. Six months in, they called to say that everything had changed and they wouldn't be needing me after all. Now, they were opting for a small ceremony at a registry office and a dinner with just a few people afterwards.

'We were just experiencing so much stress, pressure and grief from everyone,' she explained. 'We were having to make it this big, showy event, and we realized that wasn't what we wanted the day to be about.'

You can only imagine the relief they must have felt when all the big plans were shelved and they organized the small but stress-free ceremony they really wanted. I had to applaud them and their sense of perspective.

Many couples complain that they feel as if they have drifted apart in the run-up to a wedding, and it's not really surprising. As every waking moment is filled with marriage talk, suddenly quality time, non-wedding-related chat, dates, dinners and sex have fizzled out.

What's the point of organizing a ceremony to celebrate your grand commitment to spending the rest of your life together if you hardly speak, and feel like ships passing in the night? You have to find a way to spend time together, to do non-wedding-related things and to keep reminding each other why you fell in love in the first place.

Wedding Fever – How to Stay Sane

- Spend at least one night each week together where you ban wedding talk completely.

- If you find yourself arguing all the time, go away and write a list of all the reasons you decided to get married. It's about you and your husband-to-be, not one day of your lives.

- Repeat to yourself at least once a week: 'It's about being married, not the wedding.' They're very different things.

- Prioritize. It may be your big day, but you don't have to do it all yourself. Trust your fiancé or maid of honour enough to let them take care of some of the smaller details for you, and you'll soon de-stress and actually start enjoying it all again – and it will make you a happy couple when you say those vows.

- Discuss with your partner early on what he wants to be involved in. With the best will in the world, guys just aren't interested in what colour tissue paper is going to line the invitation envelopes, but they would like to help choose the band. Establish your expectations early on.

- Work out your planning style — are you a BlackBerry Babe or a Lady of Lists? Go with what works for you, and keep track of things. Knowing where you are with your plans stops you spiralling out of control.

- Beware of asking opinions from too many people. You need to decide what is important to *you*. It's nice to include people, but it is *your* wedding.

Oh yes, I could certainly dish out the advice. Isn't it easy when it's someone else's problem you need to solve rather than your own?

As 2006 came to a close, the problems that had been lurking underneath the surface for Michael and me were growing bigger and bigger, but we weren't confronting them. I didn't feel particularly loved or that Michael found me attractive, but then what could I expect? Who would want to ravage his wife when her nose is constantly stuck in her laptop and her forehead furrowed in concentration?

Desperate to stop our relationship from flat-lining, I suggested our little family of three go for a holiday over the New Year to my uncle and aunt's place in Cornwall. Jake loved it down there, because they had goats, chickens and dogs, but it had been a long, long time since Michael had accompanied us there.

However, it seemed that my plan was immediately scuppered when Michael announced that he couldn't come down with us as he needed to stay at home for another day to work. Reluctantly, I drove Jake down, and at least Michael came along the following day.

To my delight, things started to thaw between us. I'd made a conscious effort to leave my laptop behind, and the mobile phone reception at my aunt's was so patchy we were cut off.

I think we both made an effort on that holiday, and we did have a good time. There were chats over tea and toast, and evenings playing stupid games like Operation. I felt so happy that we were all laughing and enjoying ourselves.

On the drive home, Michael squeezed my knee affectionately, and I smiled at little Jake, asleep in the back of the car. I felt a glimmer of hope. 'Now we've had some time like this, perhaps we can carry on in the same way?' I thought. Surely this new year could bring fresh beginnings?

The year 2007 certainly began positively, when I was shortlisted once more for Best Planner at the Wedding Awards. This time there was a ceremony in London, which I was really excited about going to. I'd bought my outfit and some lovely new shoes and was all ready to go.

But the day before, I was struck down by a vomiting bug. Knowing to my dismay that I'd be too ill to attend, I called the organizer to apologize.

There was a pause on the end of the line before a

strangled, 'OK, let me call you back in a few moments.'

Well, a few moments later, I actually had my head back down the toilet, so Michael answered the call, to be told that, 'It would be very good if someone from TK Weddings was there, if you know what I mean . . .'

So Michael went in my place. I think he enjoyed being there and receiving the award but, strangely, he didn't make a big thing of it when he came home.

With another award in place, once again the publicity boosted our books and the jobs kept coming in.

In an unusual scenario, one of my first weddings of the year featured not only fourteen bridesmaids, but fourteen ushers to walk them out as well. Strangely, it wasn't a massive wedding: there were only around 120 guests, which is relatively small.

Well, at least it ruled out the possibility of ostracizing any friends of the bride or groom.

I've always thought the way young bridesmaids and page boys behave at a wedding is a good indication of how they will turn out in later life.

The bridesmaid is determined, she's got her pretty frock, and she's soaking up every minute of her princess moment. (She thinks it's all about her, of course, but nobody minds as she pushes her way to the front of yet another photograph.)

Then there's the little reluctant page boy being dragged down the aisle. He might as well be sticking his heels in a block of cement and crossing his arms, with that 'No, I'm not moving, and you can't make me!' look on his face – a look that the boys often perfect when they are all grown up and someone else is trying to get them down the aisle! I guess it just starts early.

We all know that teeny-tiny bridesmaids and page boys are very cute, but be warned: they're also very unpredictable. You just never know what they are going to do.

I can remember one wedding where the four-year-old page boy totally upstaged the bride by walking down the aisle like John Cleese in a *Monty Python* comedy sketch. He'd clearly been told to walk *very sloooowly* by the bride – so he duly did this, but with great big comedy steps. He was a real little crowd-pleaser, and spurred on by the titters and outright laughs at his ungainly march, he immediately launched into precocious arm movements and started strutting down the aisle as if he was dancing to 'Night Fever'. Then, when he got to the front, he did a Michael Jackson spin and pointed at the congregation.

Being so cute, he totally got away with it, even if the bride did wonder if everyone was chortling because she'd accidentally tucked her dress into her knickers. Frankly, nobody is going to be able to make an entrance after that – no matter how beautiful a bride you are.

Picking your bridesmaids is never an easy task, and you'd be amazed at the amount of friends of the bride who believe they have a God-given right to assist their friend down the aisle. The minute a wedding is announced they immediately start jostling for position, causing all sorts of internal politics between groups of friends. Suddenly, you'll hear friends exclaiming in 'I'm likely to get very offended' tones, 'Well, I hope I'm going to be your bridesmaid . . .' or 'Well, I've been your friend for longer than . . .'

Even worse, a lot of brides fall into the trap of being so excited they blurt out comments to their friends like, 'And you can all be my bridesmaids!' It might be an off-the-cuff comment, but you can guarantee that at least one of these friends will hold them to it. In fact, they're often flicking out their diaries to arrange those dress-shopping expeditions before the bride-to-be!

The cold, clinical fact is that, for every extra bridesmaid you have, the cost of your wedding rockets. As well as a dress for each one, there are the shoes, accessories, hair and make-up. It all mounts up – and very quickly.

You really don't need a huge number. It looks odd to see the bride followed by a massive squad, and it does the one thing that's forbidden at a wedding: takes everyone's eyes off the bride. The old saying is that you can count your true friends on one hand, so it's always worth trying to remember that when choosing bridesmaids.

Once you've got your dream team in place, be warned that nothing can divide a group of women like the debate over a bridesmaid's dress. So if one style doesn't suit all, then perhaps the dresses could be designed slightly differently but all in the same colour? In any case, it makes sense to let your friends have some say – if only to avoid the sulky bridesmaid who announces she'll be changing into her own dress as soon as the ceremony is over, which happened at one of my weddings.

I remember one miserable wench who made it very clear

on the wedding day itself that she didn't really want to be there. The bride, Emily, worked in the City, and had done a six-month secondment at her company's New York office. While she was there, she'd become close friends with an American girl called Nancy, who she'd flown over to be bridesmaid.

When I first met her, I was amazed. Emily was really sweet, but Nancy was every bit your archetypal City bitch – loud, overpowering and continually attached to her mobile. She was clearly looking down her nose at everyone – especially me.

On the morning of the wedding, it was clear that she expected to be able to treat me like a dogsbody. I wasn't the wedding planner, I was 'the help'.

'I didn't get my breakfast, so I want you to ask the kitchen to make an egg-white omelette,' she demanded, in her haughty Hamptons accent.

I looked at her incredulously – not even a please!

'Perhaps you could call room service,' I suggested.

'I *don't want* to phone room service,' she snapped. 'I want *you* to do it for me.'

As if I didn't have enough to do on the wedding day!

Later, after pouting her way up and down the aisle, she plonked herself down in a chair with a drink. Then, for the whole day, she was positively vile, walking around with a surly, sullen face – apart from for the photographs, of course, at which point you'd catch a glimpse of a dazzling smile, which vanished faster than the camera flash. 'I don't think much of the venue,' I heard her bitching to her boyfriend. 'I thought Emily could have had somewhere a bit flashier than this.'

And surprise, surprise, while the rest of the guests laughed and danced along to 'YMCA', she sat in the corner with a self-important look on her face. She plainly considered herself far too fabulous for such nonsense.

If she'd kept her misery to herself, it wouldn't have been so bad, but what was unforgivable was that the bride had clearly picked up on her bridesmaid's behaviour. I think by the end of the day she knew only too well that she'd chosen the wrong person.

Meanwhile, one of her other friends proved to be worth her weight in gold, spending the whole day carrying around the bride's lip gloss and hairspray and being on hand for every beautifying bathroom break. You don't need a bridesmaid when you have a friend like that.

Perhaps Emily should have taken a leaf out of Heather's book and opted for a four-legged bridesmaid that was incapable of answering back?

Heather, one of my more 'country' brides, had told me from the start that she was determined to have her dog, Betsy, at the wedding. She'd even chosen a venue based on the criteria that they allowed pets to stay in the rooms.

Hilariously, in the week before the wedding, the dog had just as much pampering as the bride. Lucky old Betsy was taken to the dog groomer where she was washed, clipped and styled. Her doggy wedding makeover included a new lead and collar, and Heather had her florist make up a lovely floral 'collar' for Betsy to wear as she walked up the aisle with the bride. It cost more than the bride's bouquet!

Bless Betsy, she did Heather proud, behaving impeccably all day (better than some of the guests, in fact). And I think the sight of a gorgeous bride in a lovely dress, complete with white wellies and pooper-scooper in hand, will stay with me for a long time.

6.
Mad Mothers

The groom's speech was perfect. He'd praised his new wife with infectious warmth and love, he'd remembered to thank the bridesmaids, and now his attention turned to the mothers.

'We wanted to give you these to thank you for all your help,' he smiled, gesturing to two ushers, who appeared, perfectly on cue, with gorgeous bouquets and passed them across the top table.

But while the bride's mother was clearly beaming with delight, the groom's mum eyed her bunch with suspicion.

'Oh,' she exclaimed loudly. 'I see I got the smaller of the two.'

Within seconds, you could see just how far in the room her barbed comment had travelled. Eyebrows shot up all round, and people whispered in disbelief. The bride and groom looked crestfallen.

I really should have known that she'd be trouble. Jean was one of those overly done-up mums who looked as if she'd just had a makeover on *Ten Years Younger*. And she seemed very demanding.

'Is there nowhere for me to sit?' she'd sulked the minute she'd arrived at the church. 'I'd like my drinks first when we arrive at the reception . . .'; 'Oh, I don't like these flowers . . .'

Welcome to the world of mad mothers.

Mother-in-law jokes are ten a penny, but if your beloved's mother, or even your own, is interfering with your big day, then it is far from funny. Dealing with a problematic mother is the last thing you need when you are already stressed, distressed and possibly bordering on deranged with the wedding arrangements. Whether it's demands that all 'her' friends be invited to the wedding – including some random third aunt who once bounced your man on her knee – or histrionics on the day, it'll be hard not to bite her head off. But the best thing to do really is to grin and bear it.

Take Tina, whose mother-in-law held up proceedings for dinner because she wanted to get changed into her evening outfit. It was rude and inconsiderate, but Tina chose to take a deep breath and carry on. Making an issue of it would only have caused tension with her new husband. Not the best way to start married life.

I've met some monster mothers in my time, but one of the worst was Jenny's mum, Yvette, who darkened my door in the summer of 2007.

Usually, 'mother interference' is a result of parents putting money towards the wedding. If Mummy and Daddy are paying, Mummy and Daddy want some say in what they're paying for, and who gets to experience it. But in Yvette's case, it wasn't even as if she was picking up the bill. Jenny and her fiancé, Doug, were paying for everything, but

Yvette still had concrete ideas about what *she* wanted and insisted that everything should be done just so.

'I want the ushers to escort myself and Doug's mother to our seats,' she announced grandly. 'It's etiquette, and it would be nice for us to make a bit of an entrance.'

It's also the easiest way to irritate the life out of the bride-to be. And, unfortunately, this time, to annoy me as well.

With Yvette, there was a constant stream of criticism. The invitations just weren't up to scratch. 'No, this just won't do,' she said. 'Why doesn't it say that your father and I "cordially" invite the guests? It has got to be changed,' she scolded Jenny.

Inevitably, the hymns that the happy couple had selected weren't good enough either.

'You can't have a wedding without "All Things Bright and Beautiful",' she blasted. 'No, I insist on that one.'

As the weeks went by, there was seemingly no subject that Yvette didn't have an opinion on. Certainly not one she could keep to herself anyway.

The number of ushers had to be the same as the number of bridesmaids so they could all walk out together, because 'It will look completely amateurish otherwise,' and she even wanted the people giving speeches to forward the drafts to her for her stamp of approval before the big day. She was a real pain. How Jenny and Doug got to their wedding day without strangling her, I have no idea, but they did.

During the wedding rehearsal, Yvette had eyed the

proceedings with the steely glare of Arlene Phillips putting on a West End production. When it came to the moment for everyone to file out of the church, she'd lined them all up and dictated exactly when she thought they should walk – and at what pace – in perfect timing to the music.

On the day, everything seemed to be going to plan, and even Yvette looked pleased – until it came to her show-stopping finale.

After the register had been signed, Jenny and Doug, giddy and elated, had made to leave the church – too early. Laughing and smiling, they began to walk down the aisle; that is, until they were stopped in their tracks by a furious Yvette, her beetroot face clashing terribly with her crimson suit and hat. Her face said it all, Jenny and Doug were speechless.

I thought I'd filled my quota of nightmare mums for a lifetime with that one. If only.

The majority of mothers don't mean to interfere. They actually mean well and just want to feel included in what they know is the biggest day of their child's life. Like all the times your mum's stepped in to help when you're struggling to cope, your wedding is no different. They think they're helping. It's just that, sometimes, they get it quite spectacularly wrong.

Feeling irritated by your partner's bossy mother, or indeed your own, is nothing new, and thankfully there are ways you can meet her halfway or tactfully stop her from completely taking over. It's all about setting the ground rules of who is the boss – and doing it early. Right from the off, you need to make it obvious that you've already decided what you're doing and to present your plans as final. By saying, 'This is what we have decided,' you are making your intentions crystal clear – that the plans are not open to discussion.

If a mother-in-law still insists on helping, then perhaps you could give her a very specific job to do. If it's early on, get her researching stationery or something similar. It will make her feel important. You could also offer to go dress shopping with her to get her outfit, or ask her to get together with your mum to organize 'photoboards' displaying pictures of you and your husband-to-be with comedy bad haircuts from your childhood, for example.

If she keeps insisting on a certain subject, then fob her off. Say, 'It's a great idea, we'll talk about it,' but then shut the conversation down. By the time you see her next, you can just pretend you forgot and say you decided to go with something else. Once the decision's made, there's not much she can do.

Rest assured, no matter how interfering your mum or mother-in-law may be, I'm pretty sure she'll pale in comparison to the bulldozing, upstaging she-devil that was Camilla's mother, Hannah.

While Camilla was a sweet, charming client, her mother was not, and it was as I was suffering from my usual winter throat plague – a horrible bout of tonsillitis – that I had my first run-in with her. The illness had rendered me unable to eat or even talk, and after a trip to A&E because my throat was so swollen I couldn't open my mouth properly, I'd emailed most of my clients to explain that I was too ill for phone calls but would still be available on email.

Most sent back sympathetic replies, but then the phone rang.

'Hello?' I just about managed to croak.

'Don't you know the wedding is in the summer?' Hannah immediately barked down the phone.

'Yes,' I croaked. 'But it's only December.'

'We need to talk about the bridesmaids *now*,' she snapped.

How she expected me to speak when I could barely breathe I'm not sure so, hamming up a coughing fit, I promised to email her and hung up. Then I constructed an email and craftily copied her daughter and soon to be son-in-law in to it.

The groom immediately emailed me back to apologize, saying that he knew I wasn't well and that he was also being screamed at. We agreed to placate her by arranging a conference call for Christmas Eve. Now she could organize and enjoy her Christmas knowing that all was 'under control'.

Hannah was fast becoming the most pushy, controlling mother I'd met, and clearly expected me to drop everything and be available day and night. The thing was, my contract was with Camilla, not Hannah.

My pet hate is when bride hangers-on try and treat you like their own personal slave. You'd be amazed at the number of mothers and relatives who attempt to piggy back off the bride and groom, trying to get you to do work for them, when they're not actually the client. Then, on the day, just as you're striving to make everything perfect for the bride, you are plagued by constant interruptions.

'Can you make me a cup of tea?' or 'Can you pop out for some cigs for me?'

Well, funnily enough, I'm trying to make sure *the bride* has everything she needs.

I remember one woman who needed to move rooms at the hotel before her wedding. Her mother, who clearly thought I was her lackey, looked at me, clicked her fingers and barked, 'Tamryn can do that. Come on, get packing!'

I looked up to see the bride mouthing, 'Sorry, Tam,' while her mother stood watching stonily, making sure nothing was missed in the frantic bag-pack.

It was the way I was ordered to do it that really bugged me. I'll happily do most things to help, and it was my standard practice at weddings to clear up the bridal suite.

Once everyone has piled into the room in the morning to change, it usually looks like a bombsite, with empty glasses and cups, discarded packets of hold-ups and towels flung everywhere. So I'd make everything look nice again, and place some wedding cake in the room for the newlyweds, along with their cards and presents. I did it because I wanted to do it, not because someone snapped their fingers at me.

If I thought I'd got rid of Camilla's mum, Hannah, by sneakily emailing the bride and groom, I was dead wrong. One night in February 2007, I was just about to fall into bed when the shrill ring of my mobile caught my attention.

'Camilla's mum' was flashing on the screen, and my heart sank. I was caught in the dilemma of whether to answer and keep her happy or leave the call and face her snippy comments in the morning. Sighing, I reached for the phone.

'Tamryn, I just had to call you. I've had the most amazing idea,' her voice blasted down the phone. From the excitement in her voice, I was clearly in her good books again. 'I want to throw a party at the house for all *my* friends and family the day after the wedding. Can you start arranging that for me, please?'

'Well, we're meeting in a few days' time, so shall we discuss it then?' I replied, hoping that this would pacify her enough that she'd end the call and let me go to sleep.

She sniffed loudly, and her tone became immediately icy. 'Weeeell, if you think it can wait until then. You're the expert. But it has to be absolutely spectacular. I want everyone talking about my party, so start thinking, and I'll be expecting your best ideas when I see you.' Then the line went dead.

I pulled a face at myself in the mirror. What an awful woman. Trying to upstage your own daughter's wedding with a knockout party the day afterwards. Nice. Collapsing on to my bed with a sigh, I wondered, not for the first time, what it was about weddings that so very often sends the mothers absolutely barking mad.

Mad mothers come in all shapes and sizes, and their temporary insanity takes many forms.

There is, however, one thing they all have in common, and that's the sudden, and often complete, loss of their grip on reality.

The Mums

The Spotlight Stealer

This mum will turn up in a bridal-style white dress, or something equally inappropriate. She wants to be escorted up the aisle by two ushers while everyone gazes in amazement. She holds up the wedding breakfast because she wants to change her outfit.

Most likely to say: 'Well, it's as much my day as it is hers.'

Power-struggle Mum

She's calling the suppliers behind her daughter's back, trying to change the plans. She knows what her daughter wants but deliberately does the opposite. She's caught giving the bride and groom evils in the wedding video.

Most likely to say: 'I wouldn't have done it like that, but there you go . . .'

Possessive Mum

This mum looks like she's mourning rather than celebrating. She constantly criticizes her child's other half, and the night before the wedding tells her son or daughter she can make it all go away. On the day, feeling defeated, she downs gins and slumps in her seat.

Most likely to say: 'You've still got time to change your mind.'

Mum in a Million

She's done everything in her power to make it a perfect day, without creating an issue of it. On the morning of the wedding, she is making everyone cups of tea and bacon sarnies and asking if they need anything. She comes well stocked with tissues and sheds tears of joy during the service.

Most likely to say: 'This is the happiest day of my life!'

I can never quite fathom what the motivation is for mums hell-bent on monopolizing their son or daughter's nuptials. Is it a longing to recapture their youth? Re-live their own wedding dreams through their children? Or simply their struggle to accept that Mummy's little treasure is finally flying the nest?

Whatever the trigger, I have seen the nicest of mothers turn into crazed hostesses, drinking themselves into oblivion by dinner or making passes at the best man. Then there are the 'Oh-so-superior' mothers who bitch incessantly about the other family and make the most indiscreet comments. Do they care if they make their own child cry on their wedding day? No sirree.

And it's not just their children or daughters-in-law they are insanely jealous of – they cannot abide the ghastly wedding planner who has stolen away their rightful job. Why pay for some stranger to organize the day when Mummy could have managed just fine?

One über-controlling mum even spent her daughter's wedding day shadowing me with her own clipboard. Did she plan to enjoy the wedding and let her hair down? Oh no, not when she could be stalking me across the room telling me how to do my job. Clipboard Mum even had a manic minute-by-minute plan of the proceedings:

1.26   *Bride and father to line up outside ceremony room*
1.27   *Tamryn's last dress check (to include laying out of train and straightening of bow on back of dress)*
1.28   *Bridesmaid last-minute-duty instruction (Please*

remind Elise which chair she should sit in, as she took mine TWICE in rehearsal)

1.29 *String quartet to begin*

1.30 *Bride and father to make way up aisle*

I begged her to go and enjoy the wedding and allow me to take the stress, but she continued to fuss, getting more and more worked up when the proceedings were out of sync with her beloved schedule. I'd already warned her that it would take longer than her allotted ten minutes to get everyone in for dinner, but she was determined not to listen.

I wasn't sure if she had extreme OCD or was just a total control freak with uncontrollable nerves, but either way, I got the impression that she needed to prove she could do better than me, and I found it increasingly difficult to operate with her constantly looking over my shoulder.

Although at first she told me I'd made a pig's ear of it all (the photos had overrun by five minutes, according to her schedule), several gins down she was on the verge of tears, begging me to employ her. 'Once this wedding is over, I just won't know what to do with myself,' she cried dramatically. After irritating me for weeks on end, I could have given her some ideas, but probably not polite ones.

To avoid 2007 passing purely in a flurry of weddings, I was trying my best to spend quality time with Michael and Jake. We'd try to have people over for dinner, or for barbecues, or plan 'family' days out. But as our little break in Cornwall became a distant memory, we started to drift apart again. All too often, something would come up that meant we'd have to cancel.

Jake was obviously our main focus, and while we both concentrated on him, we were at the same time avoiding having to deal with each other.

On one occasion, I booked a meal out for us on a Friday night, but then Michael cancelled at the last minute by text message. That was how any bad news like that was invariably conveyed. Whether Michael was working late, or had missed his flight, the news was always broken to me by text message. It was honestly as if we'd just given up, and avoiding things was easier than facing problems.

We would eat dinner on our laps most evenings, conversation unnecessary because the television would be on, and after that, Michael would sit at his laptop in the study or in the dining room. If we talked, it was about work, or about light, fluffy stuff like a silly picture in the paper. It was almost as if neither of us wanted to start a more serious conversation, because we didn't know where it would end up.

Yet I'd fob myself off with excuses. Perhaps I had too high expectations for marriage? Maybe because I saw the highs of love all the time at work I expected the same for myself, when it just wasn't real life? Perhaps I should just be grateful for the good things and not expect romance and passion? So conversations continued to revolve around work and Jake, and while it looked to people as if we had everything, it didn't take much scratching at the surface to see that things were only just being held together.

I just had no idea what to do to fix things. I was stuck in a rut and I couldn't see a way out, and while we both said nothing it couldn't cause any conflict. There were no real arguments, just sighs, stilted meaningless conversations, tears and an overwhelming sense of helplessness. It felt like a strange, slow death of a marriage.

So yet again I opted for the only coping mechanism I had – work.

And believe me, nothing can distract you more than seeing a mother arrive at her son's ceremony in a floor-length ivory dress that looked suspiciously like a bridal gown. Granted, there are some very lovely ivory dresses in the shops in the summer, but it's an unspoken (and sometimes spoken) rule that, at a wedding, it's only the bride who gets to wear white.

If this mad mother was looking for some attention, it certainly had the desired effect, not least when she deliberately chose to enter the church after everyone else was seated. When the doors opened and a woman in white began to step through, everyone turned to look – only to be greeted by the sight of the mother of the groom walking slowly down the aisle, beaming at all the guests along the way.

The poor bride – you can only imagine her face when she entered the church to see another woman in white standing at the altar with her arm around the groom. Of course, it was the talk of the wedding, as everyone tutted at her blatant attempt at scene-stealing. I'm sure any psychologist would be in their element dissecting her unconventional choice of outfit.

At the other end of the scale, there are the mothers who seem to have forgotten their age and inadvertently wander into Lipsy to purchase a dress that would make a member of Pussycat Dolls look demure. They wiggle up the aisle in their bum-skimming little numbers, tottering on their platform heels, wafting perfume and done up like a dog's dinner, making the vicar blush and the other guests wince.

WAG weddings aside, does anyone really think a leopard-print sheer fabric is suitable wedding attire? Yet I know at least two mothers who deemed it the perfect outfit in which to watch their child tie the knot.

One was the 'mutton dressed as lamb' divorced mother of the groom, who turned up in a mid-thigh-length leopard-print dress and sky-high heels. If there's a stereotypical image of a divorced woman desperately trying to roll back the years and look slimmer and younger, this mum fulfilled every cliché and then some. Her attire just screamed 'Look at me!'

It was quite clear what was going on – the groom's dad, her ex, was there with his new partner (looking very classy), while poor Mum was still single. She'd plainly decided to show him exactly what he'd turned his back on.

While she was a very attractive lady, with a great figure, the visual assault of OTT hair, fake tan, full make-up and that dress just smacked of Bet Lynch. The guests couldn't help staring, and it was only made worse when she became quite loud after a couple of drinks.

Later in the evening I saw that she was sitting on her own nursing a glass of wine, looking distinctly sad – the wide smile and overly loud laugh long gone. I think perhaps she realized she'd made a mistake and had actually only made things worse for herself. She'd put on her war paint but ended up opening herself up for more of an attack. I felt really sorry for her – she knew she'd messed up but, worse, around a hundred other people had watched her do it.

Anyway, back to the ongoing nightmare that was Camilla's mum.

Her post-wedding party was just one symptom of her ever-increasing obsession with her daughter's big day. Soon, not an afternoon went by without the dreaded call from her. Camilla was my client, yet Hannah would call me up continually, suggesting that I have 'a discreet word' with her daughter to try to dissuade her from this idea or that. She was putting me in an impossible situation. I was trying to do my job and give Camilla the wedding she wanted, but if I didn't play the game with Hannah, she'd tell Camilla that I was hopeless and still continue to make my life a misery.

There wasn't an element of the wedding that Hannah didn't want to have influence over. She booked appointments at the stationery company at times she knew Camilla wouldn't be able to make, and asked for another set of all the demo CDs from the shortlisted musicians to be sent to her.

'I just want to feel a little bit included in the decision,' she sulked down the phone to me. A little bit included? I almost choked on my coffee.

When Camilla announced she wanted to have her wedding dress made for her, Hannah called first thing the next morning.

'Tamryn, darling, I want you to find me someone to make my outfit,' she trilled. 'I've got to look amazing, because it's such an important day for me.'

You had to give her credit. The party, and indeed everything else, was a spectacular effort to upstage her daughter. I wondered how on earth Camilla would react.

'I'm just wondering if a big party the next day might be too much,' I tried to say tactfully the next time I spoke to her. 'The wedding will be a long day, and people will be tired.'

'Nonsense,' she barked. 'The hair of the dog never hurt anyone.'

I headbutted the table silently, wondering how on earth I could play this.

'Now you can give me a separate quote,' she continued. 'Cost is not a problem. I'll just have to try not to monopolize your time for *my* little party,' she added, a little too gleefully for my liking.

I had no doubt that she intended to take up as much of my time as possible.

So there I was, now contractually bound to the mother

from hell, a pathetic pawn in her battle to be the centre of attention.

Predictably, over the next few weeks, Hannah's plans became more and more indulgent. The whole house was re-arranged, complete with hired furniture and bar. Nibbles and canapés became a large buffet, with plenty of staff to pander to guests' every whim.

She wanted the wedding florist to provide another set of flowers and arrangements to make the room 'spectacular', and she thought she might make 'a little speech'. Her *pièce de résistance* came when I was sent the rather lengthy guest list. For some reason, Camilla and her new husband weren't on the list, and I assumed there must be a mistake.

'Oh no,' Hannah replied. 'I'm sure they won't want to come the day after their wedding. They'll be getting ready to go off on honeymoon.' There was a pause while she considered the one thing her daughter had organized that she was yet to trump. 'Perhaps I should take a little holiday after the party too . . .'

Well, I'm sure you can imagine how the wedding went after all of that. Hannah tested my patience every moment of the day, and I got the sneaking impression she couldn't wait for it all to be over so she could get on with the main event – her party!

Disgusted by Hannah's behaviour, I worked so hard at that wedding to make sure that Camilla got the day *she* wanted, doing more even than I usually did to make the day special for her. It went flawlessly. Everything looked beautiful, everyone was thrilled, and it was possibly one of the best weddings I've ever put together, if I do say so myself. Camilla looked radiant, and the comments she got from the guests were brilliant.

Ever the gracious bride, Camilla didn't hesitate to thank me for my contribution in making the day such a hit. I suspected that Hannah probably loathed me by the end of the day, as I'm sure she thought I'd spent way too much time with Camilla, and not enough with her – which, if I'm honest about it, gave me a little smug satisfaction.

As the new Mr and Mrs left their reception at the end of the evening to cheers, whoops and popping champagne corks, Hannah turned to me with a slightly psychotic smile and said, 'Well, Tamryn, you're going to have to work hard tomorrow to top this.' She laughed, but there was no hint of humour in her voice. There was no doubt about it, she was officially the maddest of all the mad mothers.

I would love to tell you that Hannah got her come-uppance, but I'm not sure she did. Her 'little party' went swimmingly, and the perfectionist in me couldn't help but want everything to go wonderfully, even if my devilish side was desperately shouting, 'She deserves it to be disastrous!'

Perhaps I can take a little bit of comfort from the fact that, while Camilla looked like she was carefree and truly enjoying her day, Hannah looked like she was working hard to be charming, humorous and perfect. Oh, and I can certainly be glad that when, soon after she asked me to organize her Christmas party, I could honestly say I was already booked for that date.

My main concern at that moment was trying to counter the 'silent but deadly' influence an opinionated mum was managing to exert on her daughter, despite being in the USA.

I'd certainly seen a few 'Diva Developer' mums over the years. They seemed to be more prevalent in 'new money' families where the mum probably didn't have the cash to flash at her own wedding so, my God, she's going to make up for it at her daughter's. They range in deviousness from the slightly interfering to those who are so utterly nightmarish you're convinced that, if you parted that perfectly styled hair, you'd be able to spot a set of horns peeking through.

One of the most common is the mum who sits right next to her darling girl at all the meetings, talking over her, questioning her decisions and telling her, 'You can have anything you like, darling. This is your wedding day, and it's going to be everything you want.'

When the bride has the 'go' from her mum that she can have everything, she can give in to her inner diva, knowing that her mother isn't going to disapprove. If it costs a fortune and is as flashy as a glitter ball, she'll be thrilled. Nothing must stand in the way of her baby having her dream day.

Strangely, though, in a way these overt mums are easier to deal with – at least you know what's going on, you can hear what's being said, and you can come up with a clever strategy to negate their nastiness. A bit of pandering to Mummy often works a treat, and when she thinks you're on her side, she's a pussycat.

But the Diva Developer mother that's the hardest to handle is Cassie's 'silent but deadly' type. You rarely see her, you don't speak to her but, my goodness, you certainly know about her. She's often a matriarch who can turn a sweet, happy and joy-to-work-with bride into a complete nightmare.

This mum is clever, and she knows that outright disagreement with her daughter isn't the way to get what she wants. Instead, she'll make innocent little comments such as: 'Is that the best that's on offer, darling?'; 'I like that idea, but if you did this, it would be so impressive'; or 'You only get to do this once – why not ask if there's an alternative?'

This mum knows how to keep herself out of the spotlight and away from the stress while adding to it and undermining her daughter at every turn, to the point where the bride-to-be has to turn into a diva herself in order to avoid the 'I told you so' comments from her mother.

I'd adored Cassie when we'd first met. She was lovely, really happy to be getting married, delighted to be working with me, and she had some great ideas for her day. It was easy for me to put together a plan for her that she was completely thrilled with.

She mentioned that she was going to email it to her mum ('She's feeling a little bit left out, as she's not in the country'), and that's when it all started.

Two days later I got a phone call from Cassie, and suddenly she wasn't so overjoyed with things. 'Could we look for some more suppliers?' she asked. 'Are you sure that this will work?'

Her mother had applied subtle pressure on her and, as much as Cassie had tried to stick to her guns, what good girl can go against her mum?

The problem is, the whole thing moves away from being the bride's big day and becomes everything the mother of the bride always wanted it to be. Some brides can forgive this type of behaviour, and smile as Mum stamps her authority all over the wedding, but I bet none of them truly forget it.

And it's not just the brides who can find themselves on the receiving end of Mum's wrath. Some poor grooms actually get it from both sides, being ganged up against by their intended and her mother. Suddenly, the poor groom sees flashes of his future fate, recoiling in horror as his beloved bride starts slowly to morph into her mother before his very eyes.

Egged on by Mummy, often with comments like, 'Oh, we don't need you here, this is girls' work' or 'You need another woman's opinion, darling,' the groom gets sidelined faster than a footballer with a broken metatarsal.

It's not always done in spite; it's often just because Mum and daughter are so hyped up they leave behind anyone who's not operating at their level of excitedness.

For some mums, planning a wedding is a little rite of passage, something they have to go through to be able to let go of their little girl. It's a bit like a farewell present. But it can also mean her being determined to spend as much time with the daughter in the run-up to the wedding as humanly possible.

Whatever the reason, it's easy for the poor groom to be trampled over on the way to destination Dream Wedding.

One such groom was Fergus, who I loved for his slight bumbling manner. It was very endearing, and it was clear that his bride-to-be, Lucy, loved it too.

In the lead-up to their wedding, I went to a meeting at Lucy and Fergus's home, and while Lucy and her mum were bustling around in the kitchen making tea and fetching cake, Fergus admitted to me, with slightly frightened glances over his shoulder, that he had no idea what was happening on the wedding day. 'I just don't know what Lucy and her mother are planning,' he said.

I had to feel for the poor guy. When the meeting started, Lucy and her mum sat with their matching wedding files on their knees, while Fergus looked as lost as, well, a bloke at a girls' night in.

After that meeting, I made sure I copied Fergus in on all the emails about the wedding, but I noticed that, when Lucy's mum replied, she made sure it *wasn't* sent to Fergus! At first I thought this was a genuine mistake, but when it happened again and again, I realized it was completely intended. Whether it was done with total malice, I'm not sure. Generally, Lucy's mum appeared to be very fond of Fergus, so perhaps she just thought he didn't want to be bothered with 'women's things'.

But if you let your mum leave your groom out of the arrangements, then it can lead to a whole lot of unnecessary stress. I once saw wedding-video footage of an uptight groom telling a group of children to 'shut the fuck up' in a blazing fit of rage.

The kids, being kids, were all running around outside while the photos were being set up. They were being a bit of a nuisance, but they didn't deserve the barrage of abuse suddenly blasted in their direction by the apoplectic groom. He just lost it.

'Will you buggers just fuck off!' he roared, clearly unaware that he was in video shot. 'I'm about to have a photo taken.'

Good father material? Hmm, the jury is still out on that one.

The Grooms

The Reluctant Husband

Sits there with a bored expression. He's had no involvement in decisions or planning and doesn't want to. His eyes glaze over at the mention of wedding favours. Most suppliers don't meet him until the wedding day.

Most likely to say: 'I can't say I'm that bothered really. It's just another party, isn't it?'

The Pretty-boy Groom

He wants to look as good as his bride so he does a Peter Andre, opting for hair extensions, über-white teeth and fake tan before the big day. He may even be wearing foundation, and he definitely won't be wearing a hired suit.

Most likely to say: 'Well, looking good isn't just for the ladies, is it?'

Mr Flash

He is of the attitude that you just throw money at everything. As far as he's concerned, it's not about love, it's about putting on a show of how successful he is. He grumbles about inviting her 'deadweight brother' but wants to invite his business associates. The whole thing can double up as a networking event.

Most likely to say: 'Well, it's only money, isn't it?'

Mr Bumbling

This groom means well but is a bit clueless. He turns up with his shirt hanging out and is unshaven. He's still writing his speech on toilet paper five minutes before he's due to give it.

Most likely to say: 'I don't think anyone will notice, will they?'

I also witnessed another deranged groom who had been stressed all day, going totally berserk after his beloved car was moved by a prankster.

Everyone knew that he was incredibly proud of his vintage sports car, which he'd even refer to as 'my baby', making his fiancée roll her eyes. He also made a joke in his speech about how, even though he was now a married man, he'd still have to spend some time with his much-loved four-wheeled mistress. He was still laughing at that point.

His wedding was taking place at a magnificent country house which had winding private roads leading up to it. Naturally, the groom had brought his car so he and his wife could drive off in it the following day. However, about half an hour after the first dance, I saw the groom storming through the room, a look of thunder on his face. He wasn't the kind of guy you'd mess with on a normal day, let alone on his wedding.

'Who the fuck has moved my car? Where is it?' he snarled.

There was a hushed silence as he eyeballed the guests, then, right on cue, a male guest came in, laughing triumphantly. He headed for the groom and removed a bundle of keys from out of his jacket pocket. 'I must say I've had a lovely drive around the estate,' he slurred. 'Very nice.'

The groom snatched the keys off him with a murderous look and was quickly ushered away by his bride.

If things are getting a bit strained, then it's always worth having a break, where the two of you can go off for a little wander and calm down. If he's not a social butterfly and the thought of all the mingling and chatting is driving him slowly insane, circulate together so he's not left all on his own. Have a plan for a secret sign you can make to each other that signals that you need to take a break.

Let's be honest (or should that be hopeful?), all of these relatively minor problems can be forgotten as long as the main event of the day has taken place. Wedded bliss isn't ruled out just because your man gets over-exuberant on the dancefloor. You're husband and wife, and once you've said the words and signed the certificate, all in the world should be good. So if you make it to 'I will', you're in good shape.

Doomed Grooms?

'On the morning of our wedding, my groom called me in a mad panic revealing that he'd left his suit trousers at home – 200 miles from our wedding venue – leaving me apoplectic with rage. I shouted at him that he had better get down to the high street that instant and buy or hire a new one. I cannot tell you how relieved I was to see him waiting for me at the end of the aisle, looking dapper in his morning suit.'

'My husband broke his nose in a rugby match the week before our wedding day. We spent the Saturday before the wedding, when I should have been doing all the last-minute preparations, sitting in A&E. There was horrendous swelling, stud marks all over his face and two black eyes, as well as the nose issue. On our wedding day, the swelling had gone down, and he wore a lot of make-up to cover the black eyes.'

I can remember one doomed groom who came shuffling up to me with the immortal words, 'I've had an accident . . .'

'Where?' I asked.

'Um, here,' he replied, indicating his backside.

All sorts of awful thoughts flashed through my mind until I finally grasped that he'd ripped his trousers by his crotch.

'Right,' I said. 'Come with me. I'm going to have to sew you up.'

I found a quiet room and instructed him to stand still while I crouched down behind him and quickly sewed up the offending trousers with him still in them. It could have looked very compromising if anyone had come in.

Talking of inappropriate moments, I once saw a groom kissing his mum for just a little too long. I'm sure I wasn't the only one in the room who felt quite bilious at the sight of mother and son indulging in so much fawning, kissing and face-stroking. It just looked wrong. Being Mummy's special little soldier is one thing, but when your husband-to-be is one step from Trey in *Sex and the City* and allows his mum into the bathroom to scrub his back, it's time for alarm bells to ring.

You might think those apron strings will be cut once the ring is on your finger, but don't count on it – and you have to actually make it to 'I do' first. There's a fine line between a mum who loves her boy and one who doesn't want to give him up to someone else.

I remember one mother-in-law who demanded to choose the menu for the reception meal. The way she saw it, she'd cooked all his meals from when he was a baby, so she should be able to pick what he was having for such a special occasion. It was a miracle she didn't lean over and cut up his beef Wellington for him.

The power struggle between the two favourite women in a groom's life can come in many guises. Some possessive mums just can't accept that their role as the number one woman in their precious boy's life is about to be usurped by 'that little tart'. Sounds extreme, but I've heard some mums muttering those exact words. And 'It won't last' really isn't a sentence that should ever be uttered by the groom's mother.

One bride simply couldn't stand being in the same room as her mother-in-law after putting up with years of unadulterated – well – hatred. Apparently, her husband's mum would phone the house they shared, and if her daughter-in-law answered the phone she'd hang up – only to call back a little later and have a long chat as soon as her son answered.

'I know it's her, I've done 1471,' the exasperated bride told me.

What could I do but shrug? Sometimes no amount of placating is going to fix the situation.

Another mother-in-law spent the entire wedding with a scowl on her face. Time and time again, I saw guests approach her to trill, 'Doesn't the bride look beautiful!'

And time and time again, I saw her force a constipated smile and reply, 'Hmmm, yes,' with no conviction whatsoever.

Some mums aren't so openly hostile, though – there are

those who slowly drip poison with barbed comments about the wedding plans.

'Are you sure you want that?' Mummy will ask, and woe betide the son who replies, 'Well, she wanted it.'

Cue eye-rolls from Mum, who sees this as proof that her wonderful son is being forced up the aisle by some wicked enchantress: 'See, he doesn't want to leave, really he doesn't.'

Most of the time, the bride will win out, steal the ultimate prize and actually get married – something that's just too much for some mothers-in-law to bear.

One seemed to confuse the happy day with a funeral and actually turned up in black, with a little veil on her hat. 'I am in mourning today. I am losing my son,' she announced sadly to anyone who'd listen.

You'll see and hear the mums crying during the ceremony – it's tradition. But for some of them, it's clearly not just emotion, it's loss – they're actually going through the grieving process.

Of course, my spirits were raised when I met Maria, a lovely smiley mum who, despite being on her own, had no reservations at all about her only son, Jack, flying the nest. In fact, at Jack's wedding, she literally wept for joy when she saw his bride, Francesca, walking down the aisle. Afterwards, patting her eye with a tissue, she could be heard waxing lyrical to everyone about how happy she was.

'I've always wanted a daughter,' she said, squeezing Francesca's hand. 'And now I feel like I've got one.'

The saddest mother-in-law I ever witnessed was the poor mum of the groom who spent her son's wedding day dosed up to the eyeballs on Valium.

She and her husband were paying for the majority of the wedding and hosting it at their country estate, so most of the wedding meetings took place at her home.

Initially, she struck me as someone who was just a little bit vague (things had to be repeated, and she couldn't get my name right), but she was completely charming and kind. She'd often get her groundsman to clean my car while we were having meetings, and she'd cut armfuls of flowers from the gardens for me to take home.

But, as the wedding drew closer, she grew vaguer and less in touch with reality. There were conversations about the multitude of hats she'd need for the day – a hat for the ceremony, a hat for the drinks reception – and then she wanted to change into a whole new outfit for the evening.

Then, one day, she came running through the gardens to where I was meeting with the marquee company and burst into tears. She confided that the pressure of hosting her son's wedding was getting too much and her husband wasn't being supportive. 'I don't know how I'm going to cope,' she sobbed.

I took her back into the house, made her tea and sat with her for over an hour.

She was very tearful and shaky, and told me how she was annoyed that her husband was inviting business associates to the wedding, as if it was some massive, impressive networking event. She wanted to relax and enjoy herself, but now she felt that she would be on show.

After I'd calmed her down a bit, I went home and wrote the groom a note asking if his mum was OK, because she hadn't seemed her usual self. A couple of days later, he replied to me, saying that his mum was 'a bit under the weather'. But the next time I saw her she told me that her GP thought she was depressed and stressed and had given her Valium.

'I think the wedding has made me realize that most of the happiness in my life is just a front,' she said. It was genuinely heartbreaking, and I would have done anything to help her.

On the day of the wedding, it was so sad, because she spent the entire day drugged to the eyeballs and it just looked like the spark in her had gone out. She was even vaguer than she had been when we first met, and I had to keep reminding her what was happening and what she needed to do next. I held her hand and felt her give mine a little shaky squeeze.

I even heard some of the guests discussing whether she was drunk or just rude, and I felt so sorry for her, because she was neither of those things. I really wanted to explain to people so they didn't think badly of her, but obviously I couldn't.

About three months after the wedding she sent me a beautiful thank-you letter and said that she was feeling a lot better but couldn't remember much about the day. It still upsets me now that she 'missed' her son's wedding.

My strangest wedding of 2007 had to be the one where I planned the entire day without the bride. Bizarrely, every planning meeting was with her mum and dad, who'd contacted me just after their daughter got engaged. Although I occasionally spoke to the bride on the phone and emailed her, I never actually met her – apparently because she had such a busy, high-powered job.

There's nothing much worse for a wedding planner, as so much of the job is getting a feel for the couple and what they really want from their wedding day. You develop a good understanding of the feeling they have about the day, and from that you can make decisions on the kind of wedding they would like. You watch how the bride's face lights up when a certain detail is mentioned, you look out for the telltale body language that says they're not totally comfortable with something, and you listen to every hint in their voice so as to pick up on anything that's worrying them.

Part of the enjoyment is sharing the day with someone you've built up a rapport with, but I just found this bride's mum really overbearing. I also found it very strange that the bride didn't seem to want to be involved at all – her mum literally decided everything, from the cake and the meal to the floral decorations and the DJ.

When I finally got to meet the bride on her wedding day, I was really surprised. I'd expected her to be quite a hard-nosed London lawyer type, but instead she was meek and quiet. I began to wonder if, rather than delegating her wedding to her mother, she'd had it stolen from her.

Having talked about all the mad, monstrous or meddling mothers I came across over the years, it's true to say that I also met marvellous mums in abundance, the sort of wonderful women who are kind and thoughtful and remember that this day isn't really about them.

Take my best friend Julie, whose mum spent the morning of the wedding in the hotel room where everyone was getting ready making cups of tea for the hairdresser, the make-up artist, the photographer and the bridesmaids. She supported Julie, she loved Julian, and she was utterly brilliant. It was clear that, for her, making sure everyone else was happy in turn made her happy too.

Another fab mum was Nancy, mother of the delightful Joanna.

Nancy left Joanna and Nigel to make all the decisions about their wedding. Although she gave her opinion, she always made it clear it was just an opinion, and whether they chose to listen to her or not was their prerogative. Come the day of the wedding, she could be seen laughing and smiling all the way through. Her joy was absolutely infectious.

Linda was also definitely in the 'fab mum' category. Sadly, her husband had passed away a few years previously, so she took on the job of giving Fliss away, which was just lovely. She also made her own mother-of-the-bride speech during the dinner.

She admitted that she'd never done any public speaking but, my goodness, she put her heart and soul into that speech, and there wasn't a dry eye in the house. She spoke eloquently and from her heart – there were no clichés, no trite jokes, just an outpouring of love for her husband, for Jeremy the groom, and most of all for Fliss. When she'd made her toast and sat down, there was a standing ovation from the guests. She deserved it.

7.

Something Blue

For some brides, all the trivial dramas and dilemmas fade into the background when something terrible happens. Nobody expects any kind of tragedy to hit their wedding, but when it does, you see the true strength some people have inside them.

Poor Rosie experienced every bride's nightmare when her mother passed away in the run-up to the wedding.

It all happened so suddenly.

During our first wedding-planning meeting, Rosie and her fiancé, Tom, were joined by her mum, Jan. Everything seemed fine. Jan was excited, and the four of us went through all the plans to put together a beautiful wedding. But a month down the line, everything changed.

Apparently, Jan had been suffering from headaches for some time, and had originally put it down to nothing more than migraines. But then, when her vision had gone strange one day, she'd gone to the doctor, who had referred her for hospital tests. It turned out she had an inoperable brain tumour, and the doctors didn't think she had long left.

Rosie was inconsolable. She wanted to bring the wedding forward, but Jan had begged her not to. 'Please don't,' she'd said to Rosie. 'I can still help you plan it, but you have to stick to the original plan. I don't want your wedding to be rushed, or for everyone to feel sad because of me.'

It was honestly the most heartbreaking scenario, and I admit to shedding plenty of tears over the situation.

Although she was going downhill rapidly, Jan was determined to help. She accompanied Rosie to choose her wedding dress and then, when she was too sick to leave the house, she insisted on helping from her bed. Discussing the favours and flowers when she had the strength seemed to bring temporary happiness to Jan, and to Rosie too.

As the tumour grew bigger, Jan's speech became slurred and slow, and sometimes her memory was affected, but she was still talking enthusiastically about the wedding right up until two weeks before her death.

Poor Rosie. It was such a struggle for her to carry on planning everything. I backed off and let Rosie deal with something that was obviously so much more important. All the suppliers who were working on the wedding were amazingly kind and understanding, and despite everything else that was going on, Rosie still found time to thank everyone for their help and patience. She was amazing.

Three weeks after the funeral, she found the strength to meet up with me to discuss altering some of the design plans to fit a specific theme because it reminded her of her mum.

Over the next few months, she would go through good and bad periods with her grief but, incredibly, she could always manage to put a positive light on things.

'I get through the bad bits by thinking about what Mum would want me to do,' she told me, smiling despite the tears in her eyes. 'I think about what she would say to me now.'

On the day, Rosie looked absolutely radiant. Almost everyone there knew what she'd been through and there was a real feeling of solidarity in the church, and more than a few tears in the congregation. I have never experienced anything like it. The feeling of love in that church was overwhelming.

Rather than make an issue about Jan not being there, Rosie and Tom had decided to remember her in a few silent tributes, that only those close to them knew about. I think it really helped her to do something in memory of her mum.

As well as the the various tributes, there was a picture of Jan and Rosie's dad on their wedding day next to the guest book and the newlyweds' last dance of the night was the song that had been her parents' first dance on their wedding day.

If it is possible, I'm pretty sure Jan would have been looking down smiling, and feeling justifiably proud of her wonderful daughter.

People sometimes feel they have to pay tribute to their dearly departed, but by the same token, if making a big point of your absent loved one makes you feel uncomfortable, then smaller, more subtle gestures can have just as much impact.

A quote from a beloved father on the back of the menu card will make him very much part of the day; likewise, a special brooch pinned on the bride's bouquet is a great way to incorporate a bit of family history, or to include someone in your day who can't be with you. By pinning it on the ribbon of the bouquet, the brooch is there, so you know you're carrying a piece of someone special with you, but it's done discreetly, so you don't have to explain it to anyone if you don't want to. It's there for you, and that's all that matters.

On another heartbreaking occasion, I watched as a terminally ill bride defied the odds to marry her man.

Olivia had had breast cancer once already, and everyone thought she'd beaten it, but unfortunately it had come back, and had spread. She knew she didn't have long left, but she was not going to let the disease beat her – she wanted her perfect wedding day before she died.

At first, I hadn't had a clue there was anything wrong with Olivia. She'd always been funny and upbeat in her emails, her sense of humour was wicked, and I couldn't wait to meet her. It was only when I went to her house to discuss the details of the day that I realized how ill she really was. She could barely walk, but she told me she was going to get down that aisle.

'As long as I get married, that's all that matters,' she kept telling me. The wedding was clearly keeping her going, and she was determined to make it.

I was desperate to do the best job I could for her. It seemed so unfair; she was such a lovely girl and didn't deserve to be planning her wedding under such terrible circumstances.

The day itself became one of the most moving and uplifting weddings I've ever been to. As Olivia walked down the aisle, clutching her adoring dad for support, happiness was radiating out of her. She had eyes only for her groom – and he for her.

As I wiped away a tear, it just struck me that this was what weddings were supposed to be about: pledging to love each other, no matter what the future holds.

It was obviously a huge effort for the bride, but she had a smile on her face for the entire day, and when she faltered a little during their first dance, the groom lifted her up and danced the rest of the song holding her in his arms. There wasn't a dry eye in the house.

Likewise, one of the most heartrending scenes I have ever witnessed was the little bridesmaid who was too ill to walk down the aisle but still got her magical moment.

She can't have been more than seven years old and had been really poorly all year with leukemia. Before the wedding, the bride and groom were worried she'd be too ill to make it, but despite being very sick in hospital, it was all she could talk about. So, on the day, she was allowed out of hospital and dressed in her pretty pink dress, and one of the ushers picked her up and carried her down the aisle.

She'd lost all her hair, and looked so gaunt, but the smile

of her face stretched from ear to ear. She just looked so happy, and no one could hold back the tears. We all knew it was a magical day for her and something she would always remember.

While such wedding events were moving, they were also incredibly sad, so it was with much relief that I got to witness the amazing day of Chris and Susan, which culminated in the perfect happy ending.

They were a gorgeous couple, always positive, always upbeat, with lots of ideas and a reasonable budget. But while they had all their dream plans in place, there was one problem. Chris's best man, Andy, was serving in Iraq and might not make it.

From talking to them, it was clear how badly they wanted him there. Chris and Andy had been best friends since primary school and had grown up together. Their relationship had never once faltered. At every meeting, they spoke so warmly about Andy, but it wasn't looking good. With just weeks to go, reluctantly, Chris drafted in a back-up best man.

Meanwhile, I started investigating whether there could be some kind of communication link on the day so they could speak to him. I was starting to feel like Noel Edmonds and Cilla Black all rolled into one! I wasn't sure I could quite pull it off, but I knew just how much it would mean to both of them to hear from him on their big day.

In the final weeks before the wedding, Chris was chirpy, but some of the bounce had been knocked out of him. He was so disappointed that Andy wouldn't be there.

But the day before the wedding, Chris's mum called me. 'Andy is booked on a flight to get in at 6.30 a.m. tomorrow,' she said. 'He's got to travel from Brize Norton, so he might just make it, but don't say anything. If his flight is cancelled, I don't want to give Chris false hope.'

Aaargh, the pressure! If he made it, I knew it would be the high point of their whole wedding. But if he didn't, they were bound to find out how close he'd come to being there and be crushed all over again. All any of us could do was wait and hope.

The following morning, as I was driving up to the wedding venue, my phoned bleeped. It was a text from Chris's mum: 'He's landed and is going to try and surprise them!'

I crossed my fingers and toes and tried not to let the excitement show on my face as I greeted the guests.

When I arrived at the venue, everyone was milling around. Chris seemed really perky, but still a bit sad. We could all tell that he felt there was something, or more importantly someone, missing.

He was thrilled to be getting married, but it clearly wasn't quite the same without his mate there to stand by his side. It's not just the bride who imagines their perfect wedding day, you know.

Soon it was time for the moment of truth, and as much as I tried not to, I couldn't help glancing at the door every few minutes – praying the bride and groom didn't spot me, of course!

The ceremony started, and as the vicar was welcoming

the congregation, I heard the door softly creak from my position at the back of the church. I hardly dared look, but as I turned around, a man in an army dress uniform walked in. It had to be Andy! I couldn't contain the huge smile on my face – they were going to be delighted beyond words.

He stood at the back, watching the ceremony, and it was only when the bride and groom moved across the church to sign the register that Chris looked up and clocked him.

He immediately raced down the aisle towards Andy. 'Did you see us, mate? Did you see us get married?' His grin spread right across his face.

'I did,' Andy replied, as he and Chris flew into a bear hug. 'I was here all along.'

Everyone was clapping, laughing and crying – even myself and the vicar. It was just so incredibly moving – it couldn't have been timed better in a Hollywood block-buster.

The other best man was very gracious, and only too happy to give up his position for the returning hero. 'I'm just so pleased Andy is here,' he said. 'I didn't want to make a speech, as it would have been like I was treading on his toes.'

So Andy got up and did Chris and Susan proud with an amazing, heartfelt speech.

'Well, I wrote this on the plane home,' he laughed. 'So please bear with me while I attempt to read my own handwriting.'

He looked bloody good in his army dress uniform too.

(Apparently, his dad had driven with his uniform to the church and he'd got changed in the vicar's loo!) He could have pulled about twenty times over at that wedding!

But I'll never forget the look on Chris's face as he ran back down the aisle – it would always have been the happiest day of his life, but now it was their dream wedding too, in front of all of the people who really mattered most to them.

And that's what I've realized after seeing so many people tie the knot: it doesn't matter whether the wedding is big, small, flashy or very simple; it's not about what you do, where you go or how much you spend, it's about the people there watching you promise to love each other for ever.

And so we come to every bride's nail-biter.

It doesn't matter how many weddings I've attended, the question, 'Does anyone know of any lawful reason why this couple shouldn't get married?' never fails to spark a nervous reaction in me. I suddenly find myself holding my breath and frozen to the spot, in case an accidental cough or arm spasm prompts the vicar to look my way. At the same time, my ears are pricked, listening intently, on the off chance someone pipes up and unleashes hell on the horrified couple.

I'm always asked what I'd have done if this ever happened, and my honest answer is: 'How the hell do I know?' Really, as much as I like a plan, can you ever decide in advance what you'd do about something so earth-shattering? I think not.

But, while having someone speak up and ruin a wedding at the question of 'any lawful impediment' is usually reserved for soap-opera scripts, occasionally it does happen in real life too. At one wedding, there was no reason to suspect trouble was afoot. The congregation was chirpy, the bride looked lovely and everything was happening on time. Indeed, it was all going wonderfully – until the vicar got to the killer question.

Addressing the congregation with a wide smile, he boomed, 'Does anyone know of any reasons why this couple should not get married?'

There were a few of the usual nervous giggles, but then a child's voice rang out from the back. 'Well, you don't think she's *good enough* for him, *do you*, Mummy?'

Although I couldn't see the mother in question, I could feel her shame radiating through the church.

'Well, I don't think that is quite concrete enough,' the vicar retorted, and carried on, to a few titters from the congregation.

Needless to say, the mother was completely shamed, and apparently spent the rest of the service hiding beneath her hat, absolutely mortified that private bitching in the car had now been broadcast to the entire church. Kids say the funniest things.

On another occasion, I watched in utter disbelief as a grown man, a childhood pal of the bride, sobbed big fat tears as he watched his 'friend' tie the knot. From the look on his face, there was no happiness, just complete and obvious grief that the friend he'd always secretly held a torch for was marrying someone else.

Not only was his public display of unrequited love completely inappropriate, he was sobbing unashamedly in front of the wife and children he'd insisted on dragging over from Australia with him to 'celebrate' his best friend's wedding. It was excruciating.

I did have one wedding that was called off three days beforehand.

I first met Rebecca and Stuart over lunch, and although he seemed ever so sweet, I got the impression he was slightly uninterested – a bit of a reluctant groom.

During our meeting, Rebecca was clearly taking the lead, declaring, 'I'm going to do this, I'm going to do that, I've decided . . .' while he just sat there quietly. There was no arm-touching, eye contact or little gestures between them.

I suppose I didn't give it much further thought – especially as all the meetings after that were just with the bride. There was no mistaking, though, that as the wedding loomed Rebecca was getting tenser and tenser.

'I think Stuart is finding the pressure a bit much,' she finally admitted. 'We're kind of struggling at the moment.'

Then three days before the wedding, I found a sombre voicemail on my phone from Stuart:

'Can someone call me back please,' he said. 'I've called off the wedding. What do I need to do to tell everyone else?'

All I could think was, 'Poor Rebecca'. But at the same time, I had to admire Stuart – he'd stood up, made his decision and was presumably taking all kinds of flak from all sides, but he didn't want to go through with it, and even though to just wander vaguely up the aisle would have been the easier option, he'd been true to himself, and that was quite impressive.

But it created a lot of unexpected work for us, and with no time to lose, we immediately launched into a marathon session of calling the suppliers to cancel all the arrangements.

Sadly, I never heard from Rebecca again. It was like she'd fallen off the face of the earth. The groom, on the other hand, called me quite a few times. I always felt that he was looking for approval. 'I did do the right thing, didn't I?' he kept asking me.

'Well, if you feel you have, you probably have,' I replied.

He eventually confided that it was the moment he'd picked up his suit that triggered his dramatic change of mind. 'I just thought, "If I wear this, I have to get married,"' he revealed. 'And I didn't want to get married.'

As it happened, the suppliers were fine. When you work in the wedding industry, I guess you just expect it to happen at some point or other.

One of the most horrific jilting stories I ever heard during my time as a wedding planner involved a groom completely calling it off as his bride walked towards him. My goodness, how pleased was I that that wasn't my wedding to deal with.

She was halfway down the aisle when he shouted, 'Stop, stop!'

As all hell unfolded in the church, he took all the blame, standing up and apologizing while everyone gave him an earful. Ouch.

However, it could actually have been worse. I heard one story about a guy who was actually exposed as a cheat during his wedding vows.

The love rat in question was marrying his long-term girlfriend in a civil ceremony at a stately home. It was all going smoothly, until the routine 'any lawful impediment' question. As in most services, the registrar asked in a bit of a jokey fashion, not really expecting anyone to reply.

'I have to ask,' he smiled, moving to carry on with the service.

But then, at the back of the room, there was the scraping of a chair as a young lady, a friend of the groom, stood up.

'I have something to say,' she revealed, a determined look on her face. 'He's been sleeping with *me* for the last six months.'

The poor bride-to-be looked utterly shell-shocked and, her face crumpling, she ran down the aisle, hotly followed by her bridesmaids and parents.

Meanwhile, the ghostly-pale groom sidled out another door, while his clearly aggrieved mistress made a sharp exit too. The wedding was called off, and when the groom tried to talk to his fiancée, he got a well-deserved slap across the face.

I've always wondered how someone who is cheating can

get as far as the altar. Perhaps the prospect of owning up beforehand is too much or maybe they even think their secret is safe in the hands of their lover. Either way, it's every wedding planner's nightmare, as there's nothing you can do to solve it.

In this case, the guests were ushered to the reception, where they had a few awkward drinks before leaving. Well, all apart from a token few, who immediately started to ask family members if it was OK for them to take their gifts back. There's always one, isn't there?

For a bride to be jilted in such a public way is, thankfully, very much a rarity. Even if the relationship is in trouble, most people just don't have the guts to call off a wedding at the eleventh hour. In all my wedding-planning experience, I've only had one experience of this kind of thing, and that was when I heard, weeks after a wedding, that the groom had already left his bride. Apparently, he'd known on the day that he wasn't doing the right thing, but had got so far down the line that he didn't think he could change anything.

When I look back, it was fairly obvious how unhappy he was. All day, he seemed to have his shoulders up around his head as if he was feeling really uptight, and a massive stress spot had appeared on his forehead. There'd been no bounce in his step, no infectious smile and none of those moments where you catch the groom looking at his new wife with a look on his face that says he can't believe his luck.

Where I had thought he lacked confidence in public speaking, I now realize his speech sounded so stilted because he couldn't quite bring himself to be saying the words. It's just a shame that all the expense and everyone's time was wasted – not least for his unfortunate bride.

At one wedding TK organized, we had a bad case of Chinese whispers, which got completely out of control. It was one that Julie was overseeing and, clearly, there had been some problems with the bride and groom before the big day.

In hindsight, Julie had noticed an atmosphere between the couple during their last joint planning meeting – which took place a month before the wedding and, interestingly, two weeks after Chrissy had returned from her hen do.

'They were both acting really strangely,' Julie explained. 'Chrissy had a maniacal grin on her face and seemed really OTT, while Nigel just sat there being quiet and actually quite grumpy.'

On the day of the wedding, Julie arrived early to check that everything was going OK. A couple of the bride's friends were busy helping with last-minute table decorating in the marquee, and she was intrigued to hear one girl commenting to another, 'Thank goodness it's all fine now. I was worried for a while there!'

'I know,' said the other. 'I thought I wasn't going to get to wear my hat!'

Two hours later, Julie drove to the church and joined the groom and the pack of ushers who were getting organized outside.

She was busy helping everyone with their buttonholes

when a loud voice boomed across the churchyard. It was one of the ushers, a boyfriend of one of the bridesmaids.

'Did you hear what happened on the hen night?' he was declaring to another couple of ushers. 'By all accounts, I heard Chrissy had a really good time. A *really* good time.' I don't know if he added a huge and over-the-top wink to the end of that sentence, but either way, there was no mistaking the intent in his voice.

Thankfully, the groom wasn't in earshot, and whether it was true or not, Julie was less than impressed by the usher's lack of discretion and hoped that would be the last she'd hear about it. But after the service, as people were gathering outside the church for the photos, she heard more people talking, and not lowering their voices nearly enough.

'Apparently Chrissy got up to no good in Brighton,' a woman was saying, scandalized. 'I didn't have her down as the type.'

As the next few hours passed, Chrissy's alleged indiscretion was the talk of the wedding. Champagne, canapés and gossip is obviously an absolutely addictive combination for some people. And by dinner, when the bride and groom walked in, you could see people obviously nudging each other, then pushing their heads close together and whispering.

The way people were gossiping, you'd think Chrissy had taken part in a mass orgy with six footballers. As Julie later found out, Chrissy's crime was hardly the scandal it was being made out to be. She'd got paralytic on her hen do, snogged a random bloke and, racked with guilt, had immediately owned up to Nigel. Her groom had been understandably upset but had chosen to forgive her.

It was just sad that the guy in the churchyard had blown it all out of proportion and made her sound like a complete trollop. It all seemed very mean, as the couple had clearly talked about it and sorted it out between them.

The funny thing is, brides always worry about their blokes going to stag dos – but clearly hen weekends can be just as dangerous. Yet while I'm aware of a couple of brides who had snogs on their hen dos, I get the impression that it is largely their married friends who act the worst – with premeditated plans to pull or behave outrageously.

I remember one bride's friend who was a lawyer in London but ran down a high street in Newcastle with her top off she was so drunk.

There must be other stories but I don't think people always told me the truth about their hen nights. I was like the 'wedding mum', and they assumed I might judge them on whether it was all right to be married. They wanted me to think they were perfect.

Hen-night Hysteria: True-life Confessions!

'My friend held her hen night on a party bus which took them all from bar to pub to club. She was having a whale of a time until she drunkenly fell down the steps of the bus and twisted her ankle. She spent the rest of the night sobering up in A&E.'

'I was less than impressed when my best friend announced that my hen do was the perfect pulling opportunity to bag a man. While the rest of us were chatting and having fun, her eyes were constantly scouring the club for suitable prey.'

'After a very boozy hen night in Majorca, the hen party went straight from our final night out to catch a very early flight home. The bride was so pissed that she was throwing up in a bag as we were boarding. Consequently, they wouldn't let us on the flight, and the next free one wasn't for another two days. We were all stood in the airport crying, "She's going to miss her own bloody wedding!" In the end, the nice people at British Airways took pity on us. They upgraded us, and we got home the night before.'

'I organized a hen night where the bride fell asleep at 10 p.m. and everyone wanted to go home. I clearly organize the best parties!'

'I knew a bride who went to a Greek restaurant for her hen do. Unfortunately, by 1 a.m., most of the hens were home, vomiting with food poisoning.'

'During a hen night in Dublin, I pulled an Irish hunk. I was so busy snogging him in the corner of the club that my drunken friends accidentally left without me. I was in a panic as I couldn't remember where our hostel was, but then I found a lovely taxi driver who drove me around for two hours until I found it and didn't even charge me. All the photos afterwards show me with fierce stubble rash from my snogathon.'

'I was a bridesmaid for a wedding in the summer where the hen party was the night before the wedding — not a good idea. One of the other bridesmaids got so drunk that she turned up ten minutes late for the ceremony without her dress on or make-up done. The bride was slightly stressed!'

'I went to a hen night in Manchester where we were evacuated from our restaurant. As we stood outside, a fire engine came screeching to a stop, causing much hysteria from the drunken hens. Thankfully, it was a false alarm, and after they'd given the building the all-clear, the firemen were only too happy to pose for a series of red-hot snaps with the bride!'

'My mother-in-law drank so much at my hen do that she passed out on the floor.'

I heard about one hen who decided to host a sedate dinner party at her aunt's for her hen night – only for it to descend into chaos. Meaning well, a few of her friends had thought it would be fun to organize a surprise stripper to liven up proceedings.

On the night, the guy was actually two to three hours late, and knowing that she had some sort of 'surprise' coming, the hen Felicity was clearly getting nervous. Finally, after her friend Jess made several irate calls to speed him along, this massive muscle-bound blond guy arrived and announced that he needed to get ready. Jess sneaked him upstairs and waited . . . and waited. At last she ventured into the room, to find him dressed as his alter-ego Butch 'Biceps' Cassidy in a cowboy outfit, complete with chaps and naked bum cheeks. She had no idea what he'd taken, but he seemed to completely wired and was frantically doing press-ups.

Beginning to suspect it was all a terrible idea, she coaxed him downstairs, where he set up his ghetto-blaster. Switching it on, he pumped out some kind of nasty dance version of 'Rhinestone Cowboy', which sounded like the Smurfs, and proceeded to lasso his way into the front room.

When Jess had booked him, we'd specifically asked for him to just strip and not grab anyone, but he clearly had different ideas. After running around the room manically thrusting his groin at everyone, the first person he targeted was seven months pregnant.

As he tried to straddle her, she shrieked, and the rest of

the hens yelled at him to get off. So he pounced over to the hen's aunt, a woman in her sixties, and gyrated against her. Next, he grabbed the shyest girl in the room and practically pushed his crotch in her face while placing her shaking hands on his buttocks.

'So is this a birthday?' he droned.

'No, it's a hen night,' someone snapped.

'Well, where's the bride?' he asked, but Felicity had already wisely seized her moment and dashed out of the room. With the shy girl looking close to tears, Jess stood up and started to clap frantically.

'Well, thank you, Butch,' she chirped. 'We've all enjoyed the show.'

There was a big round of applause, but Butch looked really put out. 'But I haven't even stripped yet,' he huffed as Jess ushered him out the room.

He wasn't planning to leave quietly. 'This is a rubbish hen party,' he was heard shouting at Felicity's aunt, who was trying to calm him down. 'What's wrong with you all?' Oh dear.

With the pressures of hen and stag dos, pre-wedding woes and couples who land themselves hugely in debt with their budget-busting plans, it's pretty amazing that any couple gets to the church unscathed. And even if the wedding ceremony goes smoothly, you still have the embarrassing speeches to contend with.

Most of us can recall that agonizing episode of *Friends* where, in an awful moment, on his wedding day to Emily,

Ross is heard calling her Rachel with a big goofy grin on his face. A horrifying plot from a sitcom, you might think, but just once (thankfully), I did see life imitate art.

Ironically, before her wedding, Sarah had secretly expressed her concern to me that her intended's ex-girlfriend Connie had been invited to the wedding.

'Darren is still very close to Connie,' she explained. 'She's coming to the wedding, and I feel quite uncomfortable about it.'

It was a reasonable enough thing to feel strange about – after all, who, honestly, does want to see her predecessor sitting in the church with a forced grin on her face as you make your vows?

But Sarah had even more cause for concern.

'He sometimes calls me her name by accident,' she added. 'What if he does it in the church?'

'I'm sure he won't,' I soothed. Famous last words or what!

On the big day, things appeared to be going fantastically. It was a beautiful autumnal wedding, and as Sarah made her way down the aisle, Darren looked delighted.

They exchanged vows without even a mention of the C word, and at the wedding breakfast I could see that Sarah was beginning to physically relax. When she caught my eye, she gave me the thumbs-up and a big smile.

Darren was clearly enjoying himself too. He was knocking back the champagne, so by the time it came to his speech, he'd certainly had a few. Standing up, he addressed the room with a big smile.

'Connie and I would like to thank you all for coming,' he said, gazing lovingly at Sarah.

A shocked hush came over the room, and Darren quickly turned ghost-white.

To her credit, Sarah put on a good show of indifference, laughing and commenting, 'I knew this would happen!'

Meanwhile, Connie could be seen cringing in her seat, a look of utter mortification on her face. Her boyfriend was staring at her accusingly too.

Darren tried to carry on, but it was as if he'd lost all his confidence. He rambled through his speech and finally got to the end, where he addressed the bridesmaids.

'If you guys would like to come up, Connie and I would like to give you these gifts,' he said.

Another shocked silence ensued, and while Sarah kept it together, there was no mistaking the fact she was biting her bottom lip.

Darren sat there, shame-faced and suddenly very interested in his napkin, doing his best to avoid eye contact with his newly acquired and furious father-in-law. Connie could be spied grabbing her hat and pashmina and heading for the exit, her grim-faced lover in hot pursuit.

Ten minutes later, poor Sarah could be found in the toilet crying, while an agonized Darren sat with his head in his hands outside the cubicle insisting, 'I'm sorry. I didn't mean to do it. I had the right name written down!'

They managed to make a truce in time for the first dance, but if they'd hoped to put it behind them, the groom's mates had other ideas. For the rest of the evening, they kept coming up to Darren, laughing and joking: 'Can you remember my name, mate?'

It was excruciating. You just knew it was the kind of thing that would be brought up in arguments for many years to come.

So, all round, a nightmare scenario, but it could have been easily avoided.

The fact is, Darren didn't even need to say Sarah's name out loud. The opening gambit, 'My wife and I . . .' always brings cheers and applause in a wedding speech. Also, there is nothing wrong with standing there with cards and reading aloud. Most people would rather a speech read from notes than done poorly.

I've also had to stand through (oh yes, we wedding planners aren't allowed to sit down) a couple of outstandingly awful speeches from fathers of the bride. They're obviously still very proud that their daughter got ten As in her GCSEs, but is their speech really the place to rehash her CV?

One dad droned on and on about his baby girl's work achievements for at least twenty minutes, while the guests shifted in their chairs and looked at their watches. Had he confused 'father of the bride' for 'recruitment consultant'? Was he trying to make a point that she was much more of a success than the groom, or was he just wanting kudos from the guests for fathering such a corporate success story? Who can say? But whatever he was intending, I don't think stifled yawns were part of his master plan.

True-life Wedding Speeches from Hell

'I went to a wedding where the best man's speech, told in front of the minister and the two poor old grannies, included stories about the groom having a shit in the street and being caught wanking in his room.'

'I heard about a wedding where the best man used his speech to propose to his girlfriend. Surely the biggest no-no?'

'My well-meaning friend made a bizarre tribute to his parents during his groom's speech. Addressing them across the room, he said, "Mum and Dad, I love you so much, and I just want you to know I'll put you the best care home money can buy..." Everyone laughed, but he was deadly serious.'

'My dad didn't write a speech, and he's not much of a public speaker, so my mother-in-law, who is, was feeding him lines. At one point, he got really stuck, and she said, off the cuff, "Say something about the bridesmaids being attractive." My dad dutifully said, "The bridesmaids are very attractive," at which everyone chuckled, and you could hear someone at the back say, "Isn't one of them nine?"'

'I went to one wedding where the groom was so nervous about his speech. He was shaking as he gave it, and finally sat down with a massive look of relief on his face. His bride was obviously so proud of him that she grabbed his hand and pulled him towards her for a kiss. At which, the groom accidentally whacked his champagne glass and sent a fountain of fizz all down the bride's dress.'

'At my friend's wedding, her dad was making a very heartfelt, if a little dull speech when one of the kids present flung himself across the table with a massive sigh and a loud comment of, "I'm so *boooored!*"'

Even if you are mortified by the speeches at your wedding being a bit rude, embarrassing or risqué, the chances are that everyone else will take them with the humour that was intended.

Possibly one of the most amazing speeches I heard was where the best man and the groom had been friends since childhood. The best man recounted the times they'd biked miles together, injured themselves in bouts of childhood craziness and grown up together, going in different directions workwise but never drifting apart.

This speech contained no terrible jokes, no ridiculous clichés, and it was possibly the most moving thing I've ever heard. The best man loved the groom, that was plain to see, and tears were falling down faces right across the room. When he sat down, the groom wrapped him in a huge hug, and the two of them clung to each other while everyone in the room leapt to their feet, cheering and clapping.

My friend Julie's husband, Julian, also made an absolute cracker of a speech, in which he said some fabulous things about his best man and which, again, had people dabbing at their eyes. The crowning moment of the speech came when Julian asked Gareth to come and get his present, which was revealed to be a Welsh rugby shirt that Julian had had signed by Jonathan Davies. Cue a look of total amazement from Gareth who, once he had composed himself, started his speech with, 'If Jules thinks that gift is going to stop me from embarrassing him, he's got another thing coming.'

Speech Special Touches

- Surprises during the speeches are always good, as guests get to feel they're part of a joke or special moment. Humorous photos tacked under chairs that are found at the right moment or a special gift delivered to a happy recipient brings all guests into the action.

- Ask each table to create a little wedding poem or provide them with the start of a limerick. Collect them up before the speeches, let the best man vet them (always a good idea!), and then he can read out the best ones before his toast. You can keep them all and add them to your keepsake box.

- Ask all the guests to guess the length of the best man's speech. Everyone pays 50 pence and the winner gets to choose a charity to donate it to; or forget the fee and give a bottle of champagne to the person who made the closest guess. You'll need someone to note the guesses and, of course, delegate someone responsible to time the speech.

- Make a speech yourself – stand up in front of all your wedding guests and tell your new husband just how you feel about him. Another thing that works well is for the bride to add a speech into proceedings later on when no one knows it's coming. Surprises don't have to be wildly extravagant grand gestures – just keep them a secret!

Speeches are odd things – a wedding wouldn't be a wedding without them, but it's a tough job giving one that's truly memorable (for the right reasons!). Over my years working at weddings, I've learned how to smile when I hear the same jokes over and over again, and how to frown across the room at a heckling guest to make him stop. But most of all, I've learned that all but the most awful speeches will always get a massive cheer, so take heart, wedding speech-makers – even if you're dreadful, you probably won't be made to know it.

And now on to the first dance – once a lovely opportunity to shuffle around proving that two people with two left feet really can find love, now ridiculously hyped, thanks to the rise of the YouTube video. Whether it is one couple's surprise segue from the Righteous Brothers' 'Unchained Melody' into Sir Mix-A-Lot's 'Baby's Got Back', or various versions of Michael Jackson's 'Thriller' that have made it on to the internet, the first dance has evolved.

It may be getting more and more popular to have a choreographed or gimmicky first dance, but lessons aren't cheap, and there's a lot of pressure on couples to pull off some amazing dance routine, when in fact it's something they'd never normally do.

The bad first dances are often the ones where the couple are trying too hard. If the bride is looking tense and the groom is counting, then it kind of spoils the moment and all looks a bit forced. Personally, I still think it's lovely to see people holding on to each other, just doing their thing.

A lot of people feel it has to be this big romantic moment – but it's never going to be, with a room full of people eyeballing you and flash photography blinding you.

There's plenty of room for mishaps, too.

One poor couple I heard about was left seething when the flash London DJ they'd drafted in played the right artist but the wrong song. As the bride explained, 'Throughout the dance, my husband just got more and more wound up, seething in my ear, "This song is *shit*." It was just really annoying that such a special moment was ruined by carelessness on the DJ's part.'

A good tip to ensure the same fate doesn't happen to you is to download your first dance song on to your iPod before the wedding. That way, if anything goes wrong, you can simply plug it in.

Another common dilemma is seeing the bride get caught up and nearly felled by her wedding train. If you do have a long train, it's worth asking your dressmaker to put some ties under your dress so that you can fasten it up out of the way before your dance.

To be honest, the key to making the first dance special is just to make sure it gives a real flavour of who you are as a couple. I remember one bride and groom who got on the dancefloor and the DJ put on some classical music. They stood there like they were about to begin a ballroom dance and then suddenly the track changed and they were head-banging to Metallica. It was just perfect. Their friends loved it, and it summed them up perfectly.

Another bride and groom loved to go dancing together

so, as a special treat, they employed Vincent and Flavia from *Strictly Come Dancing* to teach them their first dance. It was brilliant. Everyone knew the couple went dancing, so it really worked. They also invited Vincent and Flavia to the wedding, where they taught all the guests from eight-year-old niece to seventy-eight-year-old grandparents a special group dance. It was marvellous.

Then there were the newlyweds who led their guests outside on to the terrace of their venue, and that was where the band struck up and their dance started. The big surprise came towards the end, when the fireworks began and exploded behind the newlyweds as they whirled around.

Of course, you could go in completely the opposite direction and make it all about the comedy. Like Clara, whose husband, Ed, instructed the DJ to play a very special track for them.

As they stood there, the opening chords of 'We're Having a Gang Bang' by Black Lace blared out. All the guests were in fits as the best man joined the groom in a bride sandwich, bouncing around on the dancefloor. All the dancing lessons in the world couldn't top that.

It was as I sorted out my 2006 to 2007 company accounts that I realized my business was turning over £350,000 a year. Although the figure was breathtaking, for some reason I didn't actually feel excitement. My business success seemed like a hollow victory when I admitted the reality to myself – that my marriage was crumbling.

By now my stress levels were definitely getting worse. It wasn't just the guilt that kept me awake at night. The more successful I became, the more I realized I had to be careful.

So much was expected of me. If I organized a little picnic in the bridal suite complete with cake and champagne for one bride, then the next bride would expect that too – and more. Brides always expected more, and they wanted to feel that their planner was doing more for them than she had done for anyone else. After all, they had to be the most special . . .

I'd done well to keep my reputation in the industry squeaky clean, and I felt that everyone was just waiting for me to mess up.

I started to become obsessed with surfing wedding websites, out of complete paranoia. I'd seen wedding planners have their reputations torn to shreds on the forums, and I thought it was only a matter of time before it happened to me.

My terror was only fuelled when another wedding planner who I'd only met once put up a comment saying, 'Has anyone else had trouble getting hold of Tamryn? I've been emailing her now for three days.' It was complete rubbish, and clearly an attempt to spook my clients, but although a couple of my brides popped up to say I always got back to them, it made me extremely anxious.

It also gave Michael ammunition to pick at me. 'Can't you just leave it?' he'd complain. 'Does it matter what people say about you? What are you going to do about it anyway?'

I now felt that the bubble of indifference we'd been floating around in had burst. Now Michael seemed permanently irritated by me and seemed almost to enjoy making me miserable. I loved my husband, and all I wanted was for him to tell me I was a great mother, a good wife, and that he was proud of me. But when he snipped at me, it just made me feel so worthless. I wanted him to see how sad I was, to tell me that he adored me and wanted to make things work. It was a vicious circle. The more I moped around the house, looking hurt by everything he did or didn't say to me, the more irritating he found me.

If my mobile rang during dinner, I'd jump and answer it nervously, looking at Michael, who would make no attempt to hide the expression of annoyance on his face. He refused to understand why I always answered the phone to my clients, and if it disturbed our already silent meal, he'd slam down his knife and fork and glare at me.

'Just don't answer,' he'd say.

'I can't,' I'd protest. 'They'll just keep on at me.'

Maybe I should have been stricter about my working hours, but it was so hard. I didn't have a product to sell, it wasn't tangible, all I had was me. I relied on my reputation for being attentive, efficient and always available.

It felt like I was juggling ten balls at once, and if I let one drop then that would be it – total meltdown. I had to carry on regardless, because that's what you do. You try to make a family, you work really hard, you do the right thing, you push on. It felt like I was on a treadmill and I had to keep going – even if I was living a lie.

The worst thing was, I was constantly being called up to talk in my capacity as a wedding expert.

Sitting on the *GMTV* sofa chatting about the secrets of a successful marriage, I felt like such a fake. 'Here I am, being some big authority on marriage, yet I can't even keep my own together,' I thought silently. So I kept up the façade, smiling and reeling off perfect soundbites, even though, inside, I felt like a nervous wreck – miserable, tearful and totally on the edge.

8.
Happy Ever After . . . ?

Spouses-to-be come in all shapes, sizes and varieties. I've seen timid little women with overpowering husbands, bossy madams with shy and retiring fiancés, toyboys and cougars, sugar daddies and bottle-blonde babes, fat girls and feeders, mousy plain girls and handsome hunks, beauties and their lovable nerds, and ugly chaps who've bagged themselves a supermodel.

There are no rules: old and young, nubile and wrinkly, rich and poor, geek and chic. Opposites attract, and different nationalities and religions unite – that's just love.

But, just occasionally, you see a couple who in every way possible – personality, looks, family and background – were born to be together.

Madeleine and Dan were this couple, and just gorgeous. Dan was, frankly, a bit of an Adonis. He had been in the rowing team at uni and hadn't lost any of his chiselled perfection. Madeleine had the most glorious hair I've ever seen. I couldn't stop myself coveting her chocolate-brown curls. The two of them laughed and smiled all the time, and it was obvious they had genuine affection for each other.

And seeing them so devotedly perfect for one another was like being stabbed in the stomach.

Prior to Madeleine and Dan's wedding, I'd been doing a sterling job of putting my doubts and worries about my own marriage in a box and filing it away at the back of my mind. But then I became aware of the pure, passionate love Madeleine and Dan clearly felt for each other. I'm not sure if it was the way Dan looked into his bride's eyes as he lifted her veil for her, or the tender but passionate kiss they shared. Or perhaps it was the way they walked round the wedding venue together, never missing a moment to entwine fingers or gaze into each other's eyes.

And as if seeing the newlyweds so happy wasn't torture enough, the groom stood up to make the most amazing speech I have ever heard. It was a pure outpouring of love for the woman he adored. He said she made him a better person, that she filled him with confidence and never stopped supporting him. He talked about the way he felt when she walked into a room and how she'd surprised him continually through their relationship. And there were no lines copied from all those 'how to make a great speech' books. This was all Dan's work and, my goodness, it was impressive. But you got the feeling that Dan had not set out to impress anyone in the room but Madeleine, and I was all the more in awe of him for that.

I could feel the tears coming, no matter how much I tried to fight them. Suddenly, my cheeks were streaming, and I was caught in the dilemma of either drawing attention to myself by sniffing and wiping my face or just letting the tears continue.

I opted for the second approach, and could feel my face getting wetter and wetter, but there was absolutely nothing I could do to stop the tears. They were now completely out of my control, and my emotions had definitely got the better of me. So much for the ice-maiden persona: that was long gone now.

Most of the time, I could mute my misery. I could keep calm and carry on, staying busy, helping everyone else, smiling, smiling, smiling. But Dan's words cut me like a knife. This love nirvana, it wasn't my experience of marriage, and it never would be. I never had that feeling on my wedding day. That's not how I felt. Had I ever truly been in love?

Marrying Michael was nice, it was convenient. We'd survived for a while. I'd accepted it wasn't this huge great love. Why should it be? Some people never get that. There was no point in having such high expectations, I told myself. But in that moment, Dan's speech brought home what I was missing out on. Suddenly the state of my marriage to Michael was unbearably obvious. Inside, I felt utterly destroyed, and I knew that, for all my outward trappings of success, my life was in a shocking state.

I was still trying. Michael had home-cooked food lovingly prepared every night he was home, and I was making a real effort. It was almost as if I thought that, if I was the perfect wife, things might somehow turn around.

Now and then, I'd grasp at a little sliver of hope – like

the morning I was frantically dashing around trying to get Jake his breakfast and myself ready for an appointment with a big-budget couple.

We'd agreed to meet for a catch-up over coffee before they went to choose all the things that were going on their wedding list. Michael, completely surprising me, helpfully offered to nip to the petrol station, just around the corner, to fill up my car. I checked my watch and figured that this would save me some much-needed time, so he grabbed my keys and drove away.

Thirty minutes later, I was pacing the hallway. My husband wasn't back to take over with Jake, and I had no car. Staring out of the window, tapping my fingers impatiently and trying my hardest to hold back the tears of frustration that were threatening to come at any second, I cursed Michael. 'He must hate me,' I thought. 'Why else would he do this?'

Eventually, when Michael sauntered in, I was too mad to do anything other than grab my keys and sprint for the door. As I sped through the countryside, I pondered what on earth could be done. I didn't want to get divorced – even the idea of it made my chest feel tight. I loved Michael, and I'd married for life. Yet I could feel him slipping away from me bit by bit.

Just that week we'd had Debs and her husband, Graeme, over for dinner, and he'd disappeared upstairs for fifteen minutes. I was left alone, with a glaringly obvious gap at the table and my best friend giving me a look that spoke volumes. But I carried on, playing the hostess with the mostest and trying to gloss over the awkwardness.

When I did go up to see where Michael was, I found him in the bedroom, sitting on the bed. Was playing happy families getting that hard for him?

I just wanted Michael to look at me in the same way my grooms gazed at their brides, but that was never going to happen. Instead, little by little, Michael was completely distancing himself from me. He was shutting me off and pretending that I wasn't there. As the weeks went by, he would get home later and later from work, and leave earlier and earlier. It hurt so much that he was avoiding me, but I just didn't know what to do.

My next bride, Eva, got on my nerves a bit. Maybe I was running out of patience with ungrateful women, but her hysterics about the fact that she had become pregnant just before her wedding really grated. 'We've done it the wrong way round,' she wailed. 'Everyone will be talking about me.'

'It's not 1920 any more, you know!' I wanted to snap.

Her continuing tirade against unmarried mothers made me clench my fists and turn away from her, shaking with anger. I found it really difficult to stand there and listen – particularly as I'd had Jake out of wedlock.

To be fair, with everything unravelling at home, I didn't have the tolerance for it. I was close to losing it completely, and it would only take one more thing to push me over the edge. Counting to ten in my head, I turned round again and attempted a sympathetic smile.

'I'm pretty sure all the guests would be thrilled for you,' I said softly. 'But you could probably just keep it to yourself if you're that worried.'

So it was agreed that we'd go through a charade to cover up her happy news.

Unfortunately, the wedding fell right in the middle of a spectacular bout of morning sickness. Every time she ran to the loo to spew up that morning, we claimed it was 'her nerves'.

After the ceremony, when the champagne corks popped, it was clearly going to be harder to cover up why the bride wasn't knocking back the bubbly in celebration. To her credit, Eva actually did a good job of nursing and pretending to sip the same glass of fizz all afternoon. As she circulated and people attempted to refresh her glass, she kept smiling, 'No, no, I had one earlier. I'm trying to pace myself.' She was sticking to her plan, and even though I didn't like it, I had to admire her tenacity.

But with Eva still feeling sick and getting backache, I was a little worried about how she'd cope while the photos were being taken. There was a lot of standing up as everyone posed and rotated in and out of the group shots, so I kept passing her canapés and forcing her to eat them. 'You have to eat,' I instructed, in very much the same tone that I used with Jake when he pushed his lasagne away for the umpteenth time.

After a while, I could see she was flaking, so I announced to the photographer that everyone needed a fifteen-minute break.

'Eva, there's something I need you to look at inside,' I said, going over to her and taking her arm. Then I marched her away from the crowd for a sit down and a cup of tea (decaff, naturally).

As she nursed her mug, Eva looked at me so gratefully that I decided I did quite like her after all.

'My dress feels really tight. Do you think anyone can tell?' she questioned, running her hand down her pancake-flat belly. 'What if Chris mentions it in the speeches?'

'I really think he won't,' I assured her, but I had a little word with him anyway.

Poor Eva, she was so tired by the end of the night it was a miracle that she wasn't slumped over a table snoring by 9 p.m. She didn't do much dancing and sat down for pretty much the rest of the evening.

I don't think she enjoyed her day as much as she should have because she spent so much of it putting on an act. I wonder if she realized that as well.

But her secret was never unmasked so, to Eva, it was probably all worth it.

A few weeks after the newlyweds returned from honeymoon, they announced their happy news. 'Oh, a honeymoon baby! How lovely!' everyone chirped. I had to laugh.

But perhaps Eva had good reason to want to do 'everything right' – particularly as she wanted a church wedding.

Times may have changed, but some vicars can still be

strict, refusing to marry couples of different denominations unless one person converts, or if they don't regularly attend the church.

I worked with one couple who were desperate to get married in a particular church. When the vicar asked if there was a special reason why they so wanted to tie the knot in 'his' church, they rather naively (or perhaps honestly) admitted that they weren't religious but liked the setting and thought the church would look pretty in the photos.

The vicar told them he would be happy to marry them but they would have to attend his church regularly for six months before he would book their wedding into his diary. Funnily enough, they decided this was too much hassle, and went for a civil ceremony in a pretty country house instead which, as the groom put it, 'looked just as good without the bother'. All's well that ends well.

On the other side of the coin, I met a lovely couple who were left heartbroken after the priest at their church refused to marry them. The bride had been christened and confirmed at this church, as well as attending services when she could, but the priest refused to marry them because the groom was divorced.

I felt so sorry for them. The groom even offered to attend classes with the bride and the priest to learn more about the faith, but still they were refused. In the end, they had no choice but to have a civil ceremony in a hotel. They were devastated. It all seemed a bit mean to me, and all very lacking in 'Christian love'.

Another couple, Mike and Louise, did bag the church they wanted – if only to be left highly embarrassed by the vicar's sermon.

For some reason, he seemed to spend a slightly inappropriate amount of time talking about 'physical love' and how important it was in a relationship. He also proudly announced to the entire congregation that he and his wife of twenty-seven years still 'made time for each other'. It made my stomach lurch.

But it was when he announced that Mike and Louise were going to learn how to 'love each other' from this point onwards that the couple really began to cringe. Either he was oblivious to the fact they'd been living together for three years before the wedding, or he just really liked talking about sex.

One lady vicar caused some chuckles among the guests when she took the 'marriage is like a wedding cake' analogy way too far in her sermon. Apparently, a marriage needs time to rise and improve, you have to feed it (with brandy, Vicar?!), and it needs to be built up layer by layer. Quite sweet. But then she continued, 'The bride and groom are like the plastic figures on top of the cake,' she mused. 'Teetering on top of the wonderful creation they've made, which at any time could be eaten away from underneath them by jealousy, greed and a lack of respect for each other. Again, quite sweet – but then came the killer line: 'So Simon, don't eat away at Debbie from underneath.'

There was much tittering and stifling of laughter from

the younger guests. Gran, however, didn't notice a thing.

My own personal pet hate is the vicars or priests who use the wedding sermon to rant about how dreadful divorce is and how divorced people have 'given in at the first sign of trouble' or that they 'couldn't be bothered to put in the effort that a marriage requires'. It's just offensive, and insulting to some of the guests. You can sometimes see brides and grooms shifting about at this point, knowing they have friends or relations who are divorced. It just casts a really nasty atmosphere over the ceremony, and it's unnecessary – surely everyone's there to talk about the two people at the altar, not a random divorced couple in the congregation?

Shall we talk about love and be positive about this couple's future? No, let's lecture and patronize people without even knowing their circumstances. Yeah, that's appropriate for a happy occasion. I'd rather take the lecherous drunk guests with the wandering hands and awful breath than a morally high-handed vicar any day.

However, there are lots of lovely vicars and priests out there, the ones who really take some time to get to know the couple they're marrying and put together a sermon that's clearly just for them and mentions how they met, their hobbies or something about their personal situation. These are the smiley vicars who look genuinely happy for the couples they marry, and they're the ones that come to the reception and are seen on the dancefloor later.

It's these guys who make the weddings seem like joyous, happy, unique occasions – not just something they're squeezing in between the funeral on Friday and family service on Sunday.

After a run of about six wedding weekends in a row, I was delighted to be able to take Jake to the zoo on Saturday. It was just as we were marvelling at the penguins that I made my usual mistake of answering my phone.

It was the father of one of my brides, and he sounded murderous.

'Tamryn,' he barked. 'Why haven't the invites been sorted? They were supposed to be done yesterday. This *simply isn't good enough!*'

He ranted and raved, and could I get a word in edgeways?

It would have been nice to have been allowed a chance to explain that his beloved daughter had asked for yet more time to make up her mind about the colour of the tissue paper inside the envelopes, but there was no chance of that.

After berating me for my 'borderline incompetence', he hung up, leaving me pressing my fingers to my temples, pretty sure I had a stress headache coming on.

Jake flung his arms around me and said, 'Smile, Mummy, smile,' so I did as I was told, and we skipped off to see the gorillas.

The next call came just as we were admiring the zebras. This time it was a bride.

'Tamryn,' she said breathlessly. 'I'm just in the hairdresser's flicking through some mags. I was just thinking, I want you to get *my* wedding into *Hello!* magazine! I would just adore it if you could.'

I stood there aghast.

'Um,' I eventually answered. 'I'm afraid *Hello!* magazine only features celebrity weddings.'

I was beginning to notice that the requests from brides were getting more and more outlandish.

'Can't you just get him to cancel the other wedding?' one bride huffed when I told her the photographer she wanted was committed to someone else.

Then there was the bride who wanted to repaint a pale-green room in a stately home to pale ivory and lilac to go with her wedding scheme. Sorry, but unless you're Mariah Carey, I think the answer is no!

And how could I forget the bride who wanted her husband to arrive at the wedding by helicopter. 'I want him to look like James Bond!' she enthused.

'That's a lovely idea,' I found myself trilling. 'But I'm afraid the venue doesn't have a helicopter landing pad.'

If that wasn't bad enough, there were the brides on average budgets who wanted to book famous bands and singers, and assumed I have Westlife, George Michael or James Blunt on speed-dial and that they're dying to play one night only at the local Women's Institute hall.

I'd get requests for butterfly releases, which I don't think is a particularly humane thing to do, or to arrange for fireworks to explode as the newlyweds' car drives away – well that's doable if you can spare an extra £3,000.

These constant demands always began with two little words: *I want*:

'*I want* all my guests to wear purple and silver so they match my decorations . . .'

'*I want* to have a song written about me for my first dance . . .'

'*I want* a fly-past from the Red Arrows – and can you get them to write my name in the sky?'

It was in the summer of 2007 that I met one of the most obnoxious women I have ever come across – and, unfortunately, she was one of my brides.

From the off, Amber proved herself to be thoroughly image-obsessed. When I'd met her as a prospective client, she'd looked me up and down before proclaiming, 'I like you, Tamryn. You're not like some of the frumpy planners I met.' God forbid!

She also took great glee in revealing that she'd overlooked all her pretty friends and chosen a line-up of 'plain Jane' bridesmaids specifically to make her look good.

'I've chosen friends who are slim enough not to show me up but not so attractive that they might outshine me,' she told me proudly.

Amber, of course, had bagged herself a rich husband, and there was to be no expense spared.

While having an unlimited amount of cash to splash had excited me at one point, now it left me cold. In fact, the more I catered for huge-budget weddings, the more I began to dislike the person that I was becoming. You know something is wrong when you think it's OK to spend £12,000 on a bar for a wedding – not for the drink or the staff, but just the piece of furniture. It just made me think, 'In what life can you justify spending that sort of money?' I can think of hundreds of things that would be so much more worthwhile.

For one wedding, we actually spent £500 on ribbon, and at another the bride spotted her 'perfect' dress in New York and spent a fortune having it shipped back. And people will spend £1,000 on a cake that no one wants to touch as they are too stuffed from the meal, so it ends up uneaten and goes stale.

It's all very well spending and spending when you can afford it, but it's the couples who can't who land themselves in all sorts of trouble. They're convinced that, unless they have an extraordinary budget, their wedding won't be any good.

Bizarrely, in just a few years as a wedding planner, I noticed a stark difference in the brides I had at the end compared to the ones I'd had at the start. As celebrity culture took off and the wedding industry boomed, offering more and more options, the range of choice and competition would make the brides really stressed. When I carried out a survey of a thousand brides on my website, I was alarmed to discover that many felt that having their guests think it was the best wedding they'd ever been to was more important than how in love they and the groom seemed. But by succumbing to Competitive Wedding Syndrome, they were leaving themselves open to stress, arguments and massive overspending.

The harsh truth for many couples is that if you want to be a 'celebrity' for a day with a handmade dress, Manolo Blahniks and Tiffany jewellery, then you either need a lottery win or, at least, a second job. It's just so easy to get carried away.

I can remember one wedding where we were doing the full planning for a couple. As usual, once they'd accepted our proposal, we'd asked them to sign contracts agreeing to pay a third of our fee upfront, a third six months before the wedding and the last instalment six weeks before the big day.

They seemed very keen for us to start work, but no money had arrived, even though they repeatedly claimed to have sent the cheque. Reluctantly, I started the work, after they'd agreed to transport chunks of money to our company account so we could pay the suppliers on their behalf. I had a venue, a cake-maker, a photographer and a band all holding dates for them, on the condition that they would pay up within the next two weeks. Yet the couple kept faffing around.

It was really awkward, as without their deposit I was risking my relationship with the suppliers, and I'd spent years building it to this point.

In the end, when the money still hadn't arrived, I was left with no choice but to front them up. 'I need to know whether you can pay or not,' I said.

Suddenly, it came out that, actually, they didn't have the money to pay, and that they'd got completely carried away.

They were dreaming of an amazing wedding – but that's all it was: a dream that could never happen.

'I'm sorry, but I can't be put in a position where I lie to the suppliers,' I told them. 'I'll hand you what I've done so far, but I can no longer take on your wedding.'

While I felt sorry for them, it annoyed me that they could allow themselves to get so carried away.

Ten Ways to Create Celeb Style on a Budget

1. Posh & Becks and Cheryl & Ashley loved their thrones, and you can make your top-table guests feel special by decorating chairs with a wrap of ribbon. Recycle bridesmaids' bouquets by tying them to chairbacks for added luxury.

2. Ditch the gigantic cakes and copy stars such as Adam Sandler, who served mini doughnuts instead, or go for lots of little cupcakes, which you can order from supermarkets.

3. If you've got your heart set on a designer dress, how about looking for something pre-loved? A designer dress agency might be the ideal way to snap up something fabulous, and even some charities have departments dedicated to selling gowns that have been donated.

4. Using things twice (or thrice!) can save cash and look great. Splash out on a couple of amazing floral decorations that can be moved from the ceremony to the drinks reception and on to the dinner.

5. Celebs never forget the little details, and a few small but unique touches are a great way to make something 'ordinary' look amazing. A strawberry dropped into the cheapest fizz instantly makes it special, and a little bit of bargain-basement ribbon tied around the venue's plain white napkins brings your colour to the reception without the cost of hiring coloured linen.

6. Stars such as Seal and Heidi Klum send guests home with extravagant goodie bags. How about wrapping up any leftover cake and giving it to guests as they leave? A nice touch at no extra cost.

7. A-listers such as J-Lo might have jewellers lining up to offer gems to borrow for the big day, but most friends would love to lend their best bracelets or necklaces to you. A great way to get your 'something borrowed' – and who's not

going to love being asked? It's a huge compli-
ment.

8. If you're a celeb, you can easily afford a top
personal trainer to whip you into shape, but if
you want to tone up, get a group of friends
together for weekly walks – a mile of power
walking burns 100 calories, and time with your
friends burns stress!

9. You might not have a dreamy castle venue, but
lots of tea lights can make anywhere look better.
Line hallways, stairways and windowsills for
instant (and cheap!) romance.

10. Celebs love 'the after party', so set one up for
yourself – quietly invite your best friends back to
your room at the end of the evening for more
drinks, late-night nibbles and more laughs. Who
wants their wedding day to end?

I've always thought the most important thing for any
wedding is the inclusion of an element of the couple's
personality.

We've all got into the habit of seeing what is in
magazines and thinking, 'I have to have it.' But if you're not

a formal person, then it looks odd to shoehorn yourself into a stiff, strict or elaborate ceremony or reception. Instead, you want guests to think, 'That could only have been their wedding.'

Using a theme for your wedding has become increasingly popular over the last few years, and with good reason as it helps you bring everything together and gives a really sleek look that has real impact.

I've been to a Scottish wedding where everyone burnt off their gorgeous roast dinner with a fantastic ceilidh in the evening; and a cricket-themed extravaganza where a stuffy drinks reception and hours spent on formal photos was replaced with a cricket match and team photos. During the day, sandwiches, cakes and tea were served to all, and rows of deckchairs gave non-playing guests somewhere to sit. The match ensured all the guests got to know each other, and the sight of the bride, in her fabulous dress, running between the wickets, was unforgettable. Everyone then signed the bat instead of a guest book and it was kept as a unique souvenir of the day.

I remember one couple, Isabella and Chris, who went to town with their seaside-themed wedding: fish 'n' chips were served to guests (wrapped in newspaper, of course), and sticks of rock with the couple's names through the centre were perfect favours.

Another bride, Ellie, wanted to give all her girlie guests a bit of a treat at her wedding, so she arranged some 'powder-room pampering' for all the females. Her amazing bathroom-based beauty divas, the Powderpuff Girls, provided make-up touch-ups, quick massages and even a couple of sneaky manicures to all those in need! Everyone loved the opportunity to take a few minutes out and then hit the evening reception looking absolutely stunning.

The whole day had a lovely girlie feel to it, with bright gerberas in the bride's bouquet and as table centres, which also had more colour injected with the addition of pink cellophane and lights inside the vases. Luggage labels had been written with the guests' names and then tied on to folded napkins with hot-pink ribbon and laid on side plates. Orchids on grasses cascaded from their stacked cake. It looked amazing.

It was in July 2007 that I received an email from Sally, a bride I'd helped two years previously. It had been a lovely winter wedding, and she and her husband had seemed really happy. Now, it turned out, they were getting divorced.

'I've been meaning to tell you for ages,' she said, 'but didn't want to make you feel bad. It's nothing to do with the wedding.'

When we emailed back and forth, she explained that they'd been more mates than anything else. It all sounded very familiar.

By now, I was crying almost every night, secretly, by myself. Michael didn't want me, and my marriage was a failure.

I also felt like his little sabotage attempts were also continuing.

One night, I'd arranged to go out with Julie and Debs

for my birthday meal, and he was supposed to be coming home to look after Jake. But then he called me an hour and a half before I was due to meet my friends to say he wouldn't make it. He'd missed his flight and wouldn't be back until the next day. He didn't even apologize. I distinctly got the impression he did it to me because he could. To show me who was boss.

When I told Debs and Julie, they were less than impressed.

'It's just his work,' I found myself uttering feebly down the phone. I felt ashamed that he was treating me like this, and I wanted to save face. It was just not working, and it was getting unpleasant.

I knew that I should leave him, but I still didn't have the strength to do it. Plus, there was Jake to think about – I didn't want him getting caught in the middle of this. The thought of hurting my little boy seemed infinitely worse than any pain caused by my disintegrating marriage to Michael.

Just when I thought I couldn't feel any lower, I came across the most miserable bride I've ever seen.

There's something distinctly wrong when a bride needs to be reminded to smile for the photos on her wedding day and she and the groom walk off the dancefloor after the first dance in different directions.

The happiness had definitely bypassed this wedding, and no wonder. Just weeks before the big day, Danielle confided in me that Sam had admitted to an affair with someone else. Apparently, they'd thrashed it out, but there had been lots of debate about whether to call the wedding off. She didn't know if she still wanted to go ahead.

Before the wedding, when she'd acknowledged that she was miserable and felt compelled to carry on even though the relationship wasn't working, I wanted to tell her to save herself, but how could I? It wasn't my place.

Danielle decided she would forgive Sam and marry him, and what followed was the most uncomfortable wedding I've ever covered.

Danielle just looked desperately unhappy all day. You could see she was trying to smile, but her eyes weren't sparkling. I felt awful for her, and I was so appalled by Sam. I kept looking at him and thinking, 'How could you do that to her?'

Danielle was just so un-bridelike. There was no excitement, no laughing, no holding hands, yet her mother kept wafting around all day cooing, 'Isn't it the best wedding ever!' As she kept popping up, making little comments to me and all the guests about how marvellous the day was, I was mystified. Either she had no idea, or she was in complete denial.

Most of the other guests seemed to know, though. As soon as the meal was over, they started saying their goodbyes and began to leave, with varying excuses. You wouldn't believe the number of babysitters who were suddenly taken ill that night. I don't think anyone could stand the atmosphere one moment longer.

'What on earth has happened?' the DJ asked me,

indicating the bare dancefloor and sombre faces all round.

It could have been such a wonderful day: the venue was beautiful, everything was perfect in so many ways – but it was happening under such a cloud.

And for me, more than anything, it just served to heighten my own unhappiness about Michael. And I think it was at that moment I fell out of love with wedding planning. It was the pure horror of seeing this bride still going through with it when she and her husband had such problems.

The drive home was unbearable, as my worst thoughts about my own marriage flooded through my mind and tears began to escape as Danielle's unhappy face haunted me. Pulling over, I sat in my car, sobbing like my heart was breaking. It was just all an intensely painful reminder that my own marriage was anything but joyful.

The next day, I met Debs and Julie for coffee and promptly burst into tears again.

'That was the worst wedding I have ever been to,' I told them. 'I wanted to tell her: "Don't end up like me."'

The two of them just sat there biting their lips and shaking their heads sadly. There was no point in them telling me to leave Michael. It was just something I had to pluck up the courage to do by myself.

I suppose I still felt that I needed some sort of validation to leave Michael. Despite the fact that it wasn't working, I was married, with a son. If Jake ended up being from a broken home, then it would be my fault. Could I live with myself? And would anyone accept my leaving just because

I was unhappy? I had a great life in so many ways – was I just being stupid, selfish and really quite mad to simply walk away from it all?

But then, a few evenings later, I broke down crying and I just couldn't stop.

I was in the bedroom, sitting on the floor, wedged in between the bed and the radiator, sobbing my heart out. I was trying so hard to keep it quiet (I'd got quite good at that), but Jake came in, and the look on his face just killed me.

Rushing over, he sat on my lap, hugged me and kissed my face over and over. 'Mummy, please stop crying,' he begged.

Hugging him tightly back, I did my best, but as big, pitiful sobs escaped, I knew that the fact my five-year-old son was getting sucked into my misery meant something had to change.

So the next day, when Jake was safely at school and Michael arrived home from a business trip, I asked him to come into the front room for a conversation. As he walked into the room, he was dragging his feet. I think he knew that finally the time for the big talk had come.

'We can't go on like this,' I started. 'It's not working, is it?'

'We could talk and work it all out,' he stammered.

'No,' I said firmly. 'We don't need to talk. We need to get divorced.'

As we both sat there mutely, trying to take in the

magnitude of the moment, I felt completely numb. 'So this is it,' I thought. 'What on earth do I do now?'

The most pressing dilemma was finding a way to tell Jake without breaking his heart in the process.

The following day we sat down together and broke it to him as gently as we could.

He took it very well. There was no shouting, no tears, no slamming of doors, just Mummy and Daddy telling him they weren't going to live together any more.

'Does that mean I'll spend half of my summer holidays with you and half with Daddy?' he asked me.

'Yes, poppet, that's exactly what it means.'

'OK,' he said contentedly. 'As long as it's fair.'

That really hurt: it was anything but fair – but in his eyes, everything was fine, and that was the best I could have hoped for.

After we'd broken the news to Jake, I went to meet Debs for a coffee.

'I've decided to divorce Michael,' I told her matter-of-factly.

A look of sympathy spread across her face, and then she paused. 'Is it all right to say that I'm really relieved?' she asked tentatively.

I very nearly managed a smile. When your best friend says that when you announce you're leaving your husband, you know you're doing the right thing.

That's not to say it was easy. After we'd made the decision, Michael moved into the spare room, and night-time made me panic. As I lay there alone with my thoughts,

I'd feel anxious and nauseous, constantly grabbing for the bottles of Rescue® Remedy piling up by my bed. I couldn't sleep and I couldn't eat.

My first post-break-up wedding came two weeks later, and it was nothing short of torturous. The last thing I wanted was to watch blissfully happy people while I was falling apart. I felt awful, too, with the lack of food and sleep, but I had to go out there and put on my professional face.

I spent the day smiling nicely and congratulating people, while all the time trying to work out where I was going to move to. 'I'm leaving my husband,' I kept thinking. 'Where do I go with my little boy?'

At first I stayed in the house. We put it on the market, and Michael moved out, but then I found somewhere not far from where we were living and moved in with Jake.

We did our best to make it easy for our son. When Michael eventually got a new place and Jake wanted me to come with them to choose furniture for his new bedroom, I did. That was heartbreaking, but it was the best thing I could do for him.

My new home was near Reading, relatively close to Mum and Debs and Julie, so I felt like I had a good support network. I was still close to Jake's school and his friends, so there was as little disruption as possible. Michael, to his credit, was decent, saying that he'd make sure I was looked after in the divorce. I guess he had just felt trapped in the marriage too.

With my domestic life changing dramatically, I also

came to a big decision about my working life too. The fact was, I couldn't seek sanctuary in my job any more. It was like having a broken leg but being made to run a marathon every day. Planning perfect days for other people and listening to their happy lives and happy plans for their happy future was incredibly hard. Of course, I still had lovely clients, but who really wants a wedding planner who, behind the smile, is hiding jaded thoughts and going through a divorce?

I discussed things with Mum, Julie and Debs, who were all resounding in their agreement.

'You can't go on like this,' they said. 'You need to take a break. To find some time for you and heal.'

So in October 2007, I emailed the girls on my books to announce I was closing the business down. 'I'm sorry, but I just can't do this any more,' I explained. 'We still have weddings to do, which we will honour, but I don't intend to take on any more.'

Julie immediately called me up. 'But you've worked so hard,' she said. 'Let me take on the business and all the weddings for you. Then you can come back when you feel up to it.'

'I won't be coming back,' I assured her. 'But you can certainly take it over.'

So that's what we did. No one was let down. We simply contacted the clients and explained that the ownership was being transferred. Then I added a notice to the website explaining that it was the end of the road for me, personally.

While most of the brides were lovely, true to Bridezilla form there were a couple of monsters who deemed me to be 'the lowest of the low' for no longer wanting to work on their weddings. How could I not want to be part of their wonderful day? I must be mad – or worse, I didn't care about them.

Two of them called me up and had a go, leaving me sitting there while they ranted and raved.

'You can say what you like, but I've made a decision,' I tried to explain. 'This is the situation, and I've tried to be as fair as possible.'

But not knowing the truth, they assumed the worst – that I'd had my fun, made my money and was off to retire in the Bahamas!

Finally, my wedding-forum paranoia was justified. One bride, who had a wedding in eight months' time, wrote the most contemptible comment: 'I think it's appalling,' she ranted. 'She is so selfish and self-centred. I hope her son gets ill and dies.'

When I read that, I sat and bawled my face off. It was just appalling. That was my lowest point, but then some of the mums from Jake's school sent me flowers and made me cry all over again. While I had no empathy from some people, I'd get support in the most unlikely places from others. It was amazing.

Before I left the business for good, I had one wedding left which I'd wanted to commit to.

It was a church wedding with a reception at a local venue, with a lovely autumnal theme. The groom wore a reddy-brown cravat, and the same colour was used in all the decorations. The bridesmaid's sashes matched and even the little page boy had a waistcoat in the same material. Everything looked fabulous.

It was strange, as that day I felt like someone was smiling down on me and making sure that I'd leave with a nice wedding. The flowers looked great: tables full of russet-coloured chrysanthemums spilling out of pumpkins and then tiny pumpkins with little tea lights stuck into them. Golden-brown leaves were used as place cards with each guest's name handwritten in gold, and the napkins were tied with tiny trails of ivy. The cake had tendrils of leaves across it, and the bride's bouquet looked wildly autumnal. It was fantastic, and I felt that this was a day where I could really smile for the first time in a long while.

Everyone at that wedding behaved fantastically – there was no drunken behaviour and no bad feeling. Or perhaps knowing that this was the last time I'd ever do this made me immune to anything that was not completely perfect.

Still, it was a very emotional day for me, and in the car from the church ceremony to the venue I cried for the entire journey.

Determined to leave on a high, I blew my nose and reapplied my make-up. Then I spent the day doing my utmost to make everything special for the bride and groom.

After dinner, as I announced the first dance, I could feel butterflies in my tummy. Was this really it? My career as a wedding planner over? Suddenly, so many emotions swamped me – sadness, nostalgia, happiness and excitement for the future.

As the final bars of 'It Had to Be You' timed out, I took one last look at the bride being swirled around on the floor by her groom, a blur of ivory silk organza. They both looked so radiant, just the way newlyweds should do. Then, smiling, I walked towards the door, a new spring in my step on that autumn day . . .

Epilogue

Standing on the stage, I looked down at a sea of faces. Opening the envelope, I smiled and leaned into the microphone: 'And the title of Best Wedding Planner 2008 goes to Julie Tooby!'

Then, suddenly, there she was, my old friend and colleague Julie, on stage grinning like a loon as I passed her the trophy. It was a really lovely moment for us both. We had a hug, both of us shaking, tears in our eyes.

Since Julie had bought TK Weddings, she'd put her own stamp on the business, rebranding it, going from strength to strength, and now scooping the most coveted accolade in the business. I couldn't think of a better successor!

As we both walked back to our seats, I looked down at a beaming, proud face – my new boyfriend, Matt.

'You were big in weddings, weren't you!' he laughed, nuzzling into my neck. 'I didn't realize I'd bagged such a powerwoman!'

All I could do was grin. What a difference a year makes.

I'd met Matt ten months after splitting with Michael. After I'd licked my wounds, I'd decided I'd have a go at internet dating. I didn't want to be this broken person who sits there bleating on for ever, whingeing about how hard done by they are and how all men are rubbish. I'd had a few 'interesting' dates, but then Matt had come along.

Admitting to my former life as a wedding planner was a bit of a nightmare. It's possibly the worst thing you can tell a guy on a date, as their natural reaction is for the word 'wedding' to freak them out. You can almost see their brains racing and the phrase 'She's going to want to plan a wedding to me' passing before their eyes. I had to do a bit of reassurance that that definitely wasn't the case.

I also knew there was a lot on the internet about me, and it was nerve-wracking to think that my dates might be going home Googling me and unearthing all sorts of horrors.

I looked very different now, with longer hair – none of the short 'great for TV' styles that I'd had before. Also, that wedding-planning woman was a lot different to the person I had become.

Matt had been married before, and also had a little boy, and we originally met at the gym for a coffee. I'd just done four marathons in four days (the ideal way to get over any break-up, I think!), so he must have thought I was a bit of a nutter, but as he was into crazy endurance events too, we hit it off immediately.

Then, in June 2009, we moved in together. For the first time in years, I feel relaxed, happy and calm.

Now I've had a little time away from the crazy, hectic life of a wedding planner, I see things a bit differently.

While I don't miss working every weekend, I do miss the happiness and excitement of weddings. I suppose, in my own way, I got as much of a buzz from them as all my clients did. There is no doubt that weddings are addictive. If you go on to any wedding forum, the number of married people who are still there is astronomical. They can't leave it. That part of your life should be a transient one, but often people can't leave. There's something about weddings that completely draws them in.

In my own way, I think I was affected by wedding madness even more so than the hundreds of brides I worked with. I let my business consume me, and I forgot what my priorities should be. Was arranging chair covers for someone more important than my family, my relationships or my health? I let it come to that, and there's no one to blame but myself.

Perhaps I was partly responsible for creating Bridezillas, by pandering to their every whim and letting them get away with their mad antics for fear of losing my reputation. I let what other people thought of me become more important than what I thought of myself. And, as much as it takes two people to create a marriage, it takes two to ruin one, and while Michael wasn't perfect, neither was I. I imagine I was very tunnel-visioned about my business, and very up and down, depending on the clients I was involved with at the time.

So I'm glad I eventually made the decision to leave both the business and my marriage behind. I don't regret either. I've done more things, learned more things and seen more things than a lot of people will ever have the opportunity to. And as my lovely mum always says, 'It's all character-building, Tam.'

As trite as it sounds, I've learned you can't create, buy or fake love. I know that true love has nothing to do with where you get married, how big your engagement ring is or what your husband-to-be does for a living. I believe that love can't be analyzed too much, because when you start to pick it apart it begins to lose its magic.

I've also learned that the happiest, most radiant and most amazing brides are those who never, ever lose focus on what's important, and that's the marriage – not the cake, shoes or place cards with individual calligraphy.

I know now that while some things are nice to have at weddings, if you don't have overwhelming love for the person you're committing to, everything else is just a sideshow. It turns out I'm a complete romantic, and despite everything I've seen and everything I've experienced, I still believe in love, marriage and complete commitment to someone else. It's the purest expression of unselfishness you can have when you agree to value someone else as much as you value yourself, and if you can live by that, you'll be happier than many people.

I've learned that optimism and hope lives within everyone, and whatever people have been through, if they love and are loved, they can cope with anything. I've learned that what people love in someone else is deeper and more profound than a nice smile or long legs. And that I, like most women, can't resist a wedding. I still love looking at wedding dresses and flowers, and I get ridiculously excited when a wedding invitation plops on to the doormat.

Whatever happens at a wedding, though, it's the marriage that's the most important thing. Bruised hearts always get better, and bad times never last, particularly if you believe in love.

After going through a grieving process – I lost my business and my husband in one go – and learning how to value myself again, I can now say I'm happier today than I've ever been. I have my health, my wonderful family, some amazing friends, a fab new partner, and a son that I love more than anything in the world.

I've used what I've learned from running TK Weddings to start a new business where I'm still helping people, but I'm stricter about not letting it take over my life.

I've come very close to falling apart, but I've got more strength than I think anyone, including myself, gave me credit for.

I've met some great people and made some special friends through weddings, and I don't suppose I'll ever be able to say goodbye completely to that world. I still hear all the industry gossip and get asked for advice, but my life is different now.

If perhaps this book has brought a little bit of perspective to the crazy world of weddings, then you leave me a happy woman, and I can honestly say, 'My work here is done.' But, as I'll never be able to get rid of my love of romance or my joy at happy endings, you'll always find a secret stash of wedding magazines hidden under my bed . . .

Wedding Summary

- **The Smother Mother**: the mother who won't back off and let her daughter just plan her own wedding and keep her nose (and her unwanted opinions) to herself. She knows best, the planner knows nothing, and her daughter can't do without her.

- **Snide Maid**: the bridesmaid who spends her day looking down her nose at everyone and everything. Clearly, she could do better (if she was nice enough to bag a man, that is).

- **Fried Bride**: she's so stressed, she can't function. To Fried Bride, a wedding isn't a wedding unless you're popping Prozac and crying on your counsellor's shoulder.

- **Bleeping Beauty**: she might look like a fairy-tale princess with the beautiful dress, the perfect make-up, the gorgeous veil and tiara, but the language that comes out of her mouth when the guests' backs are turned is definitely her something blue.

- **Ring Blindness**: the engagement ring is on and, oh no, ring blindness has set in. Characterized by the bride-to-be's inability to see anything other than her wedding plans, ring blindness can often become progressively worse in the build-up to the wedding. Friends, family, everything is blotted out by the dazzle of the ring and the lure of impending wedded bliss.

- **Wed-a-geddon**: vomiting brides, nervous grooms, bitching bridesmaids, cocky best men, hopeless ushers, angry families, drunken guests, badly behaved kids and Great-aunt Ethel on the dancefloor – it's like Armageddon, only with Wed-a-geddon, you know exactly when and where it's all going to kick off.

The guest list...

Lads on Tour

These rugby-mad boys see it as just another hilarious opportunity to embarrass the groom. They have already had five pints before the service starts, and their ushering is chaotic. They try to get the groom to play drinking games, leap up and down on the dancefloor and wind up the bride about what happened on the stag do.

Most likely to say: 'He might be getting married but he's still one of the boys.'

Bridesmaid on the Hunt

She's the one who's already asked the bride for a detailed lowdown on who's single. She changes place cards so she can sit next to eligible men during dinner and jumps the highest, elbowing other girls out of the way to catch the bouquet. Makes a sudden disappearance when she gets lucky.

Most likely to say: 'He's hot. Is he single?'

Miss Envy

She sulks throughout the entire day because her boyfriend hasn't proposed yet. During the groom's tribute to his beautiful wife, she sits with her arms folded giving her boyfriend daggers. They are heard arguing outside the marquee later about his 'lack of commitment'.

Most likely to say: 'Apparently, I'm not good enough to marry. Well, one in three marriages ends in divorce!'

Kids Behaving Badly

Within five minutes, pretty dresses and crisp white shirts are coated in mud. The kids run amok, knocking things flying or crawling along the floor to put their head up the bride's skirt. They scream whenever the photographer comes near them.

Most likely to say: 'Mum, I'm *soooo* bored. Take me home before I have a MASSIVE tantrum!'

Golden Oldies

Fabulous grandparents who are game for a laugh and loving the opportunity to let their hair down. They're squiffy after half a glass of champagne and can be seen trying to jitterbug on the dancefloor later.

Most likely to say: 'I've not had this much fun in ages.'

The Greatest Dancer

Every wedding unveils a potential Michael Flatley who takes centre stage on the dancefloor – having been egged on by people who really should know better. It's like their body is trying to go in eight different directions at the same time.

Most likely to say: 'I'm auditioning for the next *So You Think You Can Dance*!'